ROUTE 116 TO SONOMA

How Your Skills, Knowledge,
& Behaviours Can Determine
Your Journey To Success

ROSS MCWILLIAM

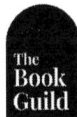

The
Book
Guild

First published in Great Britain in 2025 by
The Book Guild Ltd
Unit E2 Airfield Business Park,
Harrison Road, Market Harborough,
Leicestershire. LE16 7UL
Tel: 0116 2792299
www.bookguild.co.uk
Email: info@bookguild.co.uk
X: @bookguild

The manufacturer's authorised representative in the
EU for product safety is Authorised Rep Compliance Ltd,
71 Lower Baggot Street, Dublin D02 P593 Ireland (www.arccompliance.com)

Typeset in 12pt Minion Pro

Printed and bound in Great Britain by 4edge Limited

ISBN 978 1835741 856

British Library Cataloguing in Publication Data.
A catalogue record for this book is available from the British Library.

Sonoma Dedication

My parents, Bob & Wyn, have always been my inspiration, my guiding light, my Sonoma.

I have not always known or appreciated this, but as my life has unravelled, I have become profoundly aware of their unconditional love, honesty, consistent intent and their overwhelming belief in me.

Even after their passing, I feel this 'gift' more now than ever. I am a part of their legacy, and my legacy is to keep them in my crosshairs for the rest of my life. I want to make them proud by continually developing myself, and by so doing, I will fulfil another part of their DNA – helping others.

My beautiful niece Danni left us when she was 21, and to remember her, I want to dedicate this book to her short, but wonderful life.

Contents

Route 166 to Sonoma

Introduction

Foreword

I first met Ross during the summer of 2020 in the early months of the Covid crisis with the country locked down and people living, working and being educated in a virtual world. I'd been recommended to Ross by a mutual acquaintance as I was looking for people to appear as guest speakers for a series of virtual talks to our employees. Since that time, I've worked with Ross as he's provided mental health training to a large number of our employees, and that training has had an extremely positive impact on the people attending and the wider company.

It's been an absolute pleasure to work with Ross on a professional basis and I very much see him as a friend – he's got such a richness of experience that he effortlessly transmits to others in a genuine, personable and engaging way. Indeed, any time spent in the company of Ross is a positive experience – he will advise, inspire and motivate whilst being very authentic. Ross has really helped me overcome some personal and work challenges since we met, and his words, wisdom, insight and knowledge have also really helped me.

Throughout my life, I've read so many books and articles, particularly in relation to history, sport, high-performing teams, and leadership. I look at the shelves in my home that are stacked with such books; some gathering dust whilst others are well-thumbed.

In this book, Ross has captured the numerous learning points and advice from his experiences, and from significant others, and has brought them together into one book that provides practical advice that's simple to implement for anyone but, particularly, those young people embarking on their lives and careers who could benefit from the experiences of others.

This latest book by Ross will become very well-thumbed and will be a constant reference point as we all navigate life and take 'Route 116 To Sonoma'.

Michael Potts
European Learning & Development Manager
NTT Germany Holdings GmbH

The Rationale For The Book – The Why?

My reasons for writing this book are initially selfish. I often find writing can be quite therapeutic. So, if nobody hears my story, let alone buys the book, this writing and revealing process would have served a purpose for me. This is precisely what happened when I wrote my first five children's books. It was a way to channel my feelings around losing my mother, father and my young niece. These books are a *legacy* to my wonderful parents, and our beautiful Danni.

Beyond this personal reason, I am hopeful that through detailing the professional and personal experiences from a man in his sixties, I can offer you another way of reaching your potential and making progress in life, maybe re-evaluating or escaping your situation, or at the very least, gaining a little reprieve or respite. Maybe by offering up some insightful observations based on experience you may even challenge accepted wisdoms and received knowledge.

The book might also resonate with those who are going through pain and adversity. I have had to change, and part of that change has seen me try to come to terms with my situation. I am hopeful my insights might help others on their passage through adversity.

Over the years I have continually tried to keep growing and changing socially, intellectually, emotionally, and physically. One of the reasons behind this mindset approach is that I still believe in the game of learning and life. I am still curious to reach my own potential and find more effective ways to support myself and others.

In fact, my worsening disability made writing one of the few things I could do without pain. At first, I was a reluctant writer, but given that I spend so much time sat down, it made complete sense to maximise this time.

At an age when many people start to retire, or at least start thinking of retirement, I am still trying to work it all out actively in the professional workplace despite my health challenges. The simplest way to put this feeling is that I believe my best years are still ahead of me. If they are behind me, then I am in trouble!

The book seemed a good way of trying to capture this feeling.

If, like me, you are not a natural academic, or not even a so-called 'smart' person, then don't worry. I have tried to make the book flow, with some academic references, but I have liberally interspersed these with experiences, anecdotes and hopefully a few lines that you may find amusing.

We all have a role to play in life and everyone has something to offer. So, if *you* want to write a book, any book, don't be put off by the knowledge and expertise of others. Have belief and it will happen.

For the record, although I don't possess celebrity status, and left school with no formal qualifications, over the years I have gained various academic and CPD qualifications, probably worked or spoken in over 1,500 educational institutions, delivered training to around 500 businesses, written books, published educational articles and have appeared on various TV and radio broadcasts. Whether I am working with a five-year-old in a primary setting or those of professional post-retirement age, or everything in between such as secondary, special educational needs, highest need of emotional behavioural difficulties, trainee teachers, junior professionals, corporate executives, and established leaders – I have been in that training room. That is the strength of this book – an authentic insight into what it takes to create positive change.

As a result of these experiences and my eagerness to search out practical solutions in my work, a good friend of mine, Dr Peter Lumsden, calls me The Pracademic – I think it's a compliment.

**Ross McWilliam BA Hons,
MSc Coaching, PGCE, CMI Level 7,
MHFA England**

Sonoma

Sonoma City, Sonoma Valley and Sonoma County can all be found in California, USA. The land in the Sonoma Valley is fertile, and the climate is gentle and warm, which makes it an ideal region to grow some of the world's finest wines.

Native Americans interpreted the word Sonoma to mean '*Valley of the Moon(s)*.' Miwok legend talked about the moon '*nestling*' in the Sonoma Valley, a natural fit where everything is at peace and at one – a beautiful and natural sight (Wikipedia, March 2013).

My interpretation of this natural phenomena is that Sonoma represents:

a. Our quest to reach our potential, discover our peace, find our rightful place, to fit in, feel secure and complete.
b. This allows us to feel self-acceptance, like finding the last piece of your jigsaw.
c. Only when it is whole, are we able to fully support others on their journey.

These three components make up the Sonoma Twelve Lessons. These lessons are interrelated to each other with a natural flow. Each of the Seasons are connected.

⟨?⟩ So Why Route 116?

Route 116 is the main highway of forty-six miles that runs exclusively through Sonoma County. It starts from the north-west of the county and ends just south-west of Sonoma City. The route covers many areas of outstanding natural beauty with many memorable landscapes that have no visible intrusions. It has an aura of serenity and peacefulness.

Given this backdrop connected to Miwok legend, it seemed appropriate that 116 Sonoma Waypoint Wisdoms could be created that would allow you to reach your potential and find your way back home in life.

In *Route 116 to Sonoma* you will reach your potential and be able to bring others into play. This approach is summed up perfectly below:

"The purpose of life is to discover your gift. The work of life is to develop it. The meaning of life is to give your gift away." David Viscott (1938–1996), American Psychiatrist, Author, Businessman and Media Personality.

How To Use The Book

There are Twelve Lessons contained within the Four Seasons of life – Three Lessons per Season. Each Lesson follows a set format of:

- A short story with a hidden meaning revolving around the Lesson content.
- A global story from a known or lesser-known person or animal.

- My personal story.
- A deep dive of knowledge into the Lesson content.
- A specific famous example of an aspect from the Lesson.
- Sonoma Waypoint Wisdoms learnt in the Lesson.
- QR Code Express Conversations and Mind Exercises. This is where you can actually see examples of how to improve an aspect of performance from the Lesson.
- A Personal Sonoma Colour Profile which represents a way of measuring an aspect of your performance. (All your scores can be recorded at the back of the book where you will find the Personal Sonoma Colour Profile Matrix and an illustrative diagram which visually holds all your information.)
- Finally, in some Lessons, I have added one Challenge heading where I challenge contemporary or existing ideas based on my experiences, two Bonus Activities, three In Situ examples and four Additional Stories to further illustrate the learning.

Comparison Note

As you will find out, I am not a big believer in comparisons that seek to undermine us, be that intentionally, or otherwise, when we encounter adversity. That is why I want to remind readers that it is a pointless task adopting thinking or using phrases that seek to make somebody feel worse or grateful for their current condition.

Examples of this are: *'There is always somebody worse off,' 'You can still walk'* and *'Others are in wheelchairs'* or *'At least you're...'*

These remarks may sometimes be objectively true on the surface, but often it's not the whole picture, and very often it's subjective. These phrases exist to make somebody feel better or worse at someone's expense – it's a pointless, self-defeating exercise where nobody wins.

When you hear these phrases do you instantly feel better, has your pain gone away, has your situation changed?

Ultimately, try and seek collaboration with others who may share some experiences of adversity or disability. By supporting each other you enter into what Stephen Covey calls 'a win-win scenario' where both parties mutually benefit.

He should know what he is talking about as his book *The Seven Habits of Highly Effective People* has sold more than twenty-five million copies!

Chapters & Lessons

Chapter 1 – Spring

Lesson 1 – The Fertile Ground
Growth Mindset, Goals & Practices, Identity,
Accreditation & Self-Worth

- **Hidden Story** – Coming Last in the Desert to Win
- **Global Story** – James & the Hedge Fund Gamblers
- **My Story** – Dr Barry's Mind is Not Set
- **Deep Dive – Growth Mindset** – Dweck Mate but Only if You're Fixed;
  Mary Cai Ricci Knows Her Classroom; I Take my Hattie Off to Academic Giant, John; In Situ Accreditation – Underlay Hall Experience
- **Famous Example** – Smash it Like Martina: Game, Set & Match Acceptance; Shania is Not on the Wain
- **116 Sonoma Waypoint Wisdoms** 1-9
- **QR Code Express Conversations & Mind Exercises into...** the Balance Between Growth Mindset & Fixed Mindset
- **Personal Sonoma Colour Profile** – 1: Measurements of Growth Mindset & Self-Worth

- **My Story** – Challenging School Days
- **Deep Dive – Adversity** – There are Many Approaches
- **Deep Dive – Strengths** – How Many Neurones & Synapses do You Have?
- **Deep Dive – Mental Health** – We are All Different
- **Special Bonus Story** – The Gift of Ryan
- **Famous Example** – Don't Underestimate Wilf Paish's Stature
- **116 Sonoma Waypoint Wisdoms** 22-32
- **QR Code Express Conversations & Mind Exercises into…** Overcoming Challenges with Four Chairs
- **Personal Sonoma Colour Profile** – 3: Measurement of Strengths

Summary of Spring

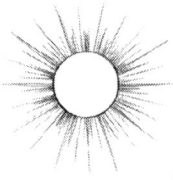

Chapter 2 – Summer

Lesson 4 – The First Flower
Custodian of Details & Laser Focus

- **Hidden Story** – Doris & Wishi, the Not So Dream Team
- **Global Story** – Nolan Kapows Batman & Wachowskis' Matrix Twin X Factor; Focus Under Pressure Neurosurgeons Help Violinist & Opera Singer
- **My Story** – PNE Trio Score a Hat Trick
- **Deep Dive** – **Custodian of Details & Laser Focus** Dr Donald Lays Down the Rules; Remember Jay Cross?
- **Famous Example** – Fred Eyre Boosts his Business With Paper Clips; Elton John is Still Standing for Details
- **116 Sonoma Waypoint Wisdoms** 33-39
- **QR Code Express Conversations & Mind Exercises into…** Remember It Like Beckham
- **Personal Sonoma Colour Profile** – 4: Measurement of Memory

Lesson 5 – A Race to Bloom
Consistency, Immediate Adaptability, Environment & Smart Resilience

- **Hidden Story** – Has the Penny Dropped for the Daughters?
- **Global Story** – Simpson Gets in a Tangle… Doh!; The Young Shuffle; Matthew Jordan Smiles Through the Rain
- **My Story** – Saudi Arabian Military Aircraft Bases – Thunderbirds Are Go!

- **116 Sonoma Waypoint Wisdoms** 45-49
- **QR Code Express Conversations & Mind Exercises into...** Active Empathetic Listening
- **Personal Sonoma Colour Profile** – 6: Measurement of Emotional Intelligence & Empathetic Listening

Summary of Summer

Chapter 3 – Autumn 🍁

Lesson 7 – Late Bloomers & Unexpected Early Wilters
Performance, Visualisation, Connectivity, Collaboration
& Vulnerability

- **Hidden Story** – The Sting in the Tale
- **Global Story** – Phelps, Watson & Macpherson Can See the End in Mind
- **My Story** – Opportunity Knocks; Tony is in the Building
- **Deep Dive – Performance** – Dr Yeung is Never Wrong; Hippo & Amy – Use Them or Let Them Destroy You; A Tip from Alan Shearer
- **Deep Dive – Connectivity & Collaboration** – Brené is Not Browned Off; Nessun Need to Worry Russell
- **Deep Dive – Vulnerability** – Surgeons – Do You Trust Them?; Anti-Heroes; Lawro Doesn't Care; An Academic Heavyweight Knows How to Get Attention & Connect
- **Famous Example** – Lucy Meacock Starts Before it Starts
- **116 Sonoma Waypoint Wisdoms** 50-58
- **QR Code Express Conversations & Mind Exercises into…** Seeing & Anchoring the Future
- **Personal Sonoma Colour Profile** – 7: Measurement of Performance Components

Lesson 8 – Expected Wilters & Evergreen Climbers
Selective Procrastination, Versatility, Clarity, Patience,
Less Intensity, Altruism & Philanthropy

- **Hidden Story** – Tom & Jerry are Like Cat & Mouse
- **Global Story** – The Colonel is Home & Fried; Taisto

- **Deep Dive – Stress Actions**
- **Flow** – Dickie Knows Best
- **Famous Example** – It's Unbelievable Jeff... Bezos Wants Harmony
- **116 Sonoma Waypoint Wisdoms** 67-76
- **QR Code Express Conversations & Mind Exercises into...** Stress Releasers
- **Personal Sonoma Colour Profile** – 9: Measurement of Flow

Chapter 4 – Winter

Lesson 10 – La Dolce Vita – A Lived Sweet Life
Integrity & Humility, Hope & Recovery, Pain & Disability

- **Hidden Story** – Dodgy Dave Learns his Lesson
- **Global Story** – Terry Can Waite a Long Time for Hope
- **My Story** – Abridged Foray Into Ross World; Siege & Crisis States
- **Deep Dive** – **Hope & Recovery** – We Must Believe
- **Deep Dive** – **Pain** – is Painful Sometimes; Dr Ingela Knows all About Pain
- **Deep Dive** – **Disability** – A Gift to Embrace or Pandora's Box?
- **Famous Example** – The Two Sirs: Tom Finney & Garfield Sobers
- **116 Sonoma Waypoint Wisdoms** 77-86
- **QR Code Express Conversations & Mind Exercises into…** Surfing Above the Pain Wave
- **Personal Sonoma Colour Profile** – 10: Measurement of Qualities & Skills

Lesson 11 – Winter's Flowering Perennials
Renewed Aspiration & Reinvention, Reflection & Feed-
forward, Expediency & Facilitation

- **Hidden Story** – Winter Breeze Jasmine in my Mind – Be More Like Eddie & The Stones
- **Global Story** – 'Aaay' the Fonz, Betty is All White & Susan is a Jewel
- **My Story** – Canada Calling for Elite Performers

- **Deep Dive – Feed-forward & Reflection –** The Dragons & John Harvey-Jones are Trouble… Shooters!; Boris Takes Bobby's Bait – Check Mate for The West
- **Deep Dive – Expediency –** Chairman Bryan is in Charge, but Teachers are Not
- **Deep Dive – Facilitation –** Face to Face or Online but Don't Attempt the Temple Pose; Richard Askam is the Perfect Facilitator, Jenny & Oshor are Super-Facilitators & Mindset Don Lifts People
- **Deep Dive – Online Facilitation**
- **Famous Example –** Roman Abramovich, Jose Mourinho & Joe Cole
- **116 Sonoma Waypoint Wisdoms 87-96**
- **QR Code Express Conversations & Mind Exercises into…** Thinking Ahead & Remembering Behind
- **Personal Sonoma Colour Profile –** 11: Measurement of Qualities & Skills

Lesson 12 – Time Immemorial
Grief & Loss, Perspectives on Life & Death, Succession & Legacy

- **Hidden Story –** Jonny & Jenny React Differently to Bruno
- **Global Story –** Different Perspectives on Death
- **My Story –** The Books are the Legacy for Dad, Mum & Danni
- **Deep Dive – Legacy –** What is Yours?
- **Deep Dive – Living Legacy Challenge –** Before it's Too Late
- **Deep Dive – Famous Legacies**

- **Deep Dive – Succession** – Brothers in Arms, Moyes & Fergie
- **Famous Example** – It Ain't Half Hot, Windsor
- **116 Sonoma Waypoint Wisdoms** 97-105
- **QR Code Express Conversations & Mind Exercises into…** Legacy and Which Animal are You… Really?
- **Personal Sonoma Colour Profile** – 12: Measurement of Life & Death

Winter Summary

Prologue

- Do you ever feel stuck, tired, unfulfilled, frustrated or even slightly down?
- Do you have a diagnosed illness or disability that has your attention, either intermittently, or 24/7?
- Do you feel neglected or even abandoned?
- Does your opinion of yourself seem to work against you sometimes?
- Are you fighting a battle nobody else knows about, or even cares about?
- In your search for a better life, are you constantly comparing yourself to others, or against your own high standards?
- Do you want to get in a good groove, be settled and in a place where you can enjoy life and all that it has to offer?
- Do you want to do more to help loved ones?

Whether you are fully engaged with life or not, these questions and accompanying emotions may arise from time to time, and this can be quite a natural occurrence as we flow through different emotional states in our professional and personal lives.

Having experienced many of these thoughts and feelings myself, I wanted to share my viewpoint on navigating through them. Our thoughts and emotions drive us, consciously and subconsciously. This does not have to be a bad thing as if we can harness our emotional energy it can be a force for positive change. The difficulty is being consistent, and when we waver or lose focus it can leave us wanting and vulnerable.

You may never win all of life's battles, but I believe success is about how prepared you are before it, how you adjust during the conflicts and how you learn from both your successful and unsuccessful experiences. Sometimes you may even have to accept or yield along the way. The human instinct though is to survive, thrive and then, if possible, support others.

I invite you to interrogate and digest the information provided, to zoom out from time to time to see the bigger picture, and simply reflect. Whether you are just starting out on your journey, are a seasoned professional who is trying to gain an edge, have started to stall in your career, or someone who wants to maximise their Winter – this book will serve your purpose.

Everyone's start and journey through life is different. We cannot make assumptions about others, but I try to live by the following four principles, as I believe everyone wants:

- To be listened to
- To be understood
- To be cared for
- To be loved

I will endeavour to do this throughout this book, and with any future correspondence you may wish to enter into.

As my good friend of forty-odd years, Peter Chester, put it: *"The book is a fascinating blend of gentle Psychology and insightful Philosophy."*

Spring

A time when the bee is pollinating and bringing life into the world. A time when the child is curious, full of hope and exploring the world with wide open eyes with no filter of judgement on what is seen or experienced. When parents, carers, teachers and grandparents recognise the need to sow the seeds of learning, trust and support within a secure and safe framework that allows the child to explore life's rich offerings.

A time, on your journey to Sonoma, educationally and holistically, to delicately foster:

- Identity
- Accreditation
- Aspiration
- Belonging
- Self-Worth
- Growth Mindset
- Capabilities
- Bravery
- Trust
- Confidence
- Strengths

- Leadership
- An Awareness of Mental Health

A time when, if adversity is experienced, the negative impacts of this can be profound, exponential even, and can last a lifetime. Conversely, in others, it can give rise to a strength that can be equally profound, and also last a lifetime.

Often, it is the interpretations and experiences in this Season, for better or for worse, that can be the template for how the child approaches and ultimately maximises the future Seasons.

"Nothing ever seems impossible in Spring, you know."
LM Montgomery (1874–1942). Author of *Anne of Ingleside* (Novel 6 of the Anne of Green Gables series).

Lesson 1:

The Fertile Ground

Growth Mindset, Goals, Practices, Identity,
Accreditation & Self-Worth

Hidden Story – Coming Last in the Desert to Win

A King had twin sons, Asif and Iqbal. He had brought up his sons with love, unconditional support, and a shared acceptance and buy-in of home and 'life' rules. Each son was supported in challenges at home, and in school, and each received praise and accreditation upon completion of challenges, be they successful or not.

When a challenge was overcome, the King would invite each son to examine what caused this success and how this could be used in future challenges. He would congratulate them. When a challenge defeated the sons, the King would ask each son where they could improve and what could be done differently next time to avoid failing. He would still congratulate them on not giving up and trying to find answers.

He instilled in them a sense of Growth Mindset where he asked the sons to demonstrate a curiosity to solve problems, a willingness to put in effort and practice, an ability to accept advice and feedback from trusted others, and to show resilience by not giving up. This application of a Growth Mindset was done in a way to encourage openness, to breed an inquisitive mind, to build in a relish for challenges, but in a way that didn't undermine the confidence of each son.

Each son still had their own identity and way of doing things. In fact, he taught them so well, that each son often looked forward to 'failure' as this led to more enhanced learning. Without knowing it, the King was embedding a sense of self-worth, identity, accreditation, belonging, curiosity and an overall Growth Mindset where 'failure' was just another step on the way to success in the future.

The King, with all his wisdom, was approaching old age. As such, he wanted to establish which son would inherit his Kingdom upon his death, so he set both sons a challenge. Each son was to leave their home and find a hidden hoard of treasure in a far corner of the desert. They could ride a camel of their choosing and the winner would be the one whose camel came back last!

What did the winner do to win the race and secure the Kingdom?

Both sons chose a camel each and raced off to find the treasure. At first, they went together. After several hours of unfruitful searching, they decided to search alone. Almost immediately, the treasure was found by Asif who then raced to find Iqbal.

Asif had a cunning plan. Upon reaching his twin, he told Iqbal he could have the treasure if they exchanged camels.

Iqbal agreed and basked in the glory of holding the treasure. Meanwhile, Asif raced back home. On entering his home without the treasure, Asif stood in front of his father and declared himself the winner and new owner of the Kingdom. His father didn't say a word, and after a few minutes Iqbal returned triumphant with the treasure in his grasp. With a smile on his face Asif declared:

"Iqbal, you might have returned with the treasure, but the camel, the one you are riding now, was mine and it came back last!" (Adapted Popular Mechanics, 2017).

The moral of the story might be that to be successful you must possess a Growth Mindset of being curious and eager to learn from successes and failures. You may also have to be resilient and possess a goal, and a desire to match that goal. It might also be about being cunning and swapping camels!

Global Story – James & the Hedge Fund Gamblers

James Altucher is an American hedge fund manager, author, and latterly podcaster and blogger (a hedge fund is a pooled investment fund that trades in relatively liquid assets and often uses high risk investment strategies). To date, he has founded twenty companies and seventeen have failed! He is a prolific writer with twenty books to his name. His podcasts have been downloaded over forty million times. He is a much sought-after business analyst with many high-profile people and organisations coveting his views and expertise. His journey has been an entrepreneurial rollercoaster, with several lows to match the highs.

After graduating in Computer Sciences from Cornell University, New York in 1989, he secured employment working for HBO. In his own time, he set up his own web design business called Reset Inc. In 1998 he left HBO and sold his company for fifteen million dollars and used this to fund other internet investments. However, over the next two years he lost it all through a series of bad decisions that left him with just one hundred and forty-three dollars and an unhealthy interest in suicide. This led him to re-evaluate his approach to business and life.

From 2002, he slowly picked up the pieces by writing about stocks for Jim Cramer and he also started trading hedge funds for large organisations. In 2006 Altucher founded the financial social network website Stockpickr. A year later, after being named one of *Times Magazine's* Fifty Best Websites, he sold the website company for ten million dollars.

Since then, he has been a seed investor in up-and-coming companies, before reaping financial rewards from the sale of such companies, sometimes with sales in excess of seven hundred and fifty million dollars! When I last looked him up he was a National Chess Master and part-owns a stand-up comedy club in New York where he also performs. (https://en.wikipedia.org/wiki/James_Altucher)

His journey has been one of developing his talents and abilities, being prepared to learn and listen, taking some high risks, but being able to reinvent himself and bounce back from severe disappointments – all traits of a classic Growth Mindset. His focus these days has shifted away from money to self-worth and his identity and accreditation comes from himself now, rather than from the business world.

So, how did he become successful, especially after so many setbacks, and become an advocate for growing his mindset?

Goals & Practices

It all starts with identifying your goals. Without goals, where are you going, and how will you know when you get there? Just floating, or drifting, means you are wasting time and motivation. It is like a tide that will soon be receding – you must take it when it's at its peak for maximal returns, or at the very least, just take it.

James Altucher's three goals are:

1. I want to be happy.
2. I want to eradicate unhappiness in my life.
3. I want every day to be as smooth as possible – no hassles.

(James Altucher Blog, 2023).

To achieve these goals he has a Daily Practice that has four components. When he does each of these four components, he usually achieves success or bounces back from a failure.

Daily Practice: A. Physical; B. Emotional; C. Mental; D. Spiritual.

A. Physical – Doing some form of exercise for about thirty minutes a day. Not to get ripped, but to get healthy. His preferred exercise is yoga as he believes if he can breathe easy when his body is in pain, then it is easier to breathe in difficult situations. This helps his mind deal with anxieties better.

He wakes up between 4am and 5am, goes to sleep between 8.30pm and 9pm and does not eat after 5.30pm.

"You can't be happy if you're not healthy."

B. Emotional – If someone is holding him back, he cuts them out of his life with no exceptions for class or status. Nobody is sacred. These people take energy out of him, and he doesn't even explain when he drops them from his circle:

"Explaining is draining."

If someone lifts him up, he brings them closer. He also believes in honesty with people. This manifests itself in only doing things that he enjoys. For example, he never attends weddings.

C. Mental – Every day, he writes down his ideas. When it starts to hurt his head that's his own sign to write down another five more. His thinking behind this is that the ideas muscle in the brain shrinks within days if you don't use it, and can take between three – six months to rebuild after it has withered.

D. Spiritual – He likes to pray, even just for a few seconds each day and be thankful and grateful in his prayers. He tries to be grateful by visualising all his friends and business colleagues, and he uses this visualisation to forgive others.

He meditates, specifically, mini-meditations for a few seconds at a time as meditations can be quite taxing, but are hugely beneficial. He studies something each day. *"When I do my daily practice I usually achieve my three goals, and that is when the magic happens!"*

He admits that it's difficult to do these four things every day, but when he does, his day goes better.

Having read all of the above, and researched James Altucher, I find his information simple, but worth adopting. Like many habits, it does revolve around being consistent, which is something we will explore later in the book. Yet, I wonder:

Would you drop a close friend or even a family member if they were draining you?

My Story – Dr Barry's Mind is Not Set

Back in 2012 I visited Professor Barry Hymer at The University of Cumbria. Barry was, and still is, an expert in Growth Mindset and his work often overlaps with that of Professor Carol Dweck whose work we will see later. I had politely asked him if I could seek his opinion on working for Osiris Educational (an independent provider of training for UK schools and colleges) and whether I would be a good fit and did I have the ability to step up into this role. He had scheduled forty-five minutes with me, and we ended up talking for ninety minutes.

I initially thought Barry had insulted me. He had done some research on me prior to our meeting, and was keen to listen to my thoughts, to ascertain exactly who this limping, enthusiastic fifty-one-year-old was before him. As we got onto the topic of Growth and Fixed Mindsets, Barry started to pick at me in terms of my academic ability and skills… or so I thought.

"Ross, you seem to struggle with some concepts, missing the detail initially. But I have noticed that your questions and appetite to understand allow you to catch up and eventually grasp the knowledge. This may ultimately see you overtake others.

I have also noticed from your books, that you are resilient and like a challenge, such as passing academic exams or dealing with your knee injury. In fact, you positively thrive on the challenge of passing something and maybe revel in the thought of proving other people wrong, especially those who may doubt you and your work. You're a classic Growth Mindset!"

I interrupted Barry curtly, sensing he was putting me down:

"Barry, I know I am no academic giant, but often with time I can pick up the thread of an argument or theory. It just takes me a few attempts."

"Absolutely, Ross, I was actually complimenting you. We all learn and process differently, and you recognise your weaknesses, but build on your strengths of perseverance, resilience, questioning, and sometimes patience!" said Barry, smiling wryly.

It was in that moment the penny dropped. I knew I was not an academic genius, but over the years I had learnt how to apply myself to achieve my goals and gain some success, in my academic qualifications, and in my professional work. Barry was recognising my struggles, but also highlighting my long-term strengths and perhaps my ability to revel in proving people and systems wrong. He was referring to my Growth Mindset. It was a moment where a serious academic heavyweight accredited me. There are moments in life where we receive accreditation. Often this is via exams and unreserved praise. That moment of accreditation felt like the equivalent of gaining a degree.

I walked out of that meeting with my head held high, my self-worth boosted, and with a steely determination to carry on writing my books, delivering training and seeing how far I could go professionally. I am still writing and training today, years after that meeting.

I am particularly proud that I have written extensive Growth Mindset courses for national training organisations such as Osiris and Creative Education, and have delivered CPD Growth Mindset training to over five thousand staff and fifteen thousand pupils.

P.S. Barry kindly wrote forewords for two of my books, and endorsed this book, so I must have impressed him on some level.

Deep Dive – Growth Mindset – Dweck Mate but Only if You're Fixed

Growth Mindset was a term first coined by Professor Carol Dweck (2006), and it was used to describe somebody who thought their skills, talents, abilities, and intelligence were not fixed or set in stone – they could always be improved. On the other hand, somebody who possessed a Fixed Mindset saw their skills, talents, abilities, and intelligence as fixed or set in stone – they could never be improved. Most people are predominantly one or the other, but some, up to fifteen per cent, can be both.

Through her research with primary-aged schoolchildren with different abilities, from different backgrounds, and from different parts of the USA, she noticed that many children initially possessed a Growth Mindset, i.e. they were curious about the world and sought to develop and grow, and believed that most things were possible.

One such experiment involved over two hundred schoolchildren. All of them were given a series of questions to answer, and from the results she graded their ability, but crucially, randomly assigned them to two groups based on nothing but luck.

Group One were labelled the 'clever group' and Group Two were labelled the 'hard-working group'.

Next, both groups were given a choice: did they want a harder test or an easier test. Only seventy per cent of the 'clever group' opted for the harder test, while over ninety per cent of the 'hard-working group' opted for the harder test.

Dweck realised that once someone is given a label they can conform to their own and other people's expectation of that label. More of the 'clever group' chose the easier test as they did not want to fail, and they wanted to keep their clever status. More of the 'hard-working group' took the harder test as they wanted to either prove they were hard-working or were not bothered about failing. They just wanted to have a go at learning.

Both groups were then given the same test (no choice).

What Dweck didn't tell the children was that there were no answers to the questions, i.e. it was impossible to answer. Initially, the 'clever group' really attacked the questions, showing great energy and optimism that they would find the answers and beat the 'hard-working group'. When no answers were forthcoming, she noticed that the 'clever group' started to go quiet and introverted, almost ashamed they could not get the answers quickly.

They started to compare with the 'hard-working group' who were not scared of failing, who were sharing ideas and were almost enjoying the challenge of proving they were hard-working. The 'clever group' gave up the test at twelve minutes, while the 'hard-working group' went on for seventeen minutes – a real triumph of perseverance and resilience whilst not being scared of what others might think.

The final test was similar to the first test, which was measuring their academic ability. When this final test was marked, she observed a clear change of individual scores from the first test. Twenty per cent of the 'clever group' had scored worse in this second test (compared to their scores in the first test), while nearly thirty per cent of the 'hard-working group' had scored better in the second test (compared to their scores in the first test).

Those who believed 'clever' labels, were falling into Fixed Mindset, while those who believed 'hard-working' labels, were falling into Growth Mindset.

To develop Growth Mindset, Dweck suggested the following ideas to children, parents and carers:

1. Encourage children to demonstrate five learning qualities:
   - Be open to failure as it is all part of a journey. Do not let peers scare you from failing. FAIL = First Attempt In Learning.
   - Put in effort and practice.
   - Be resilient by trying to solve problems and challenges.
   - Seek feedback.
   - Share learning.

2. Praise the process not the outcome. It's about the journey not the destination.

Be specific with praise, i.e. *I liked your working out, I liked the way you kept going, I liked the way you asked for guidance, feedback and support, I liked the way you shared your answers with others, I liked the way you sought to understand the question better, I liked the way you kept learning even when you didn't get the answer right.* This approach instils a sense of ongoing achievement, and there is always more to learn.

Don't keep saying, *'I think you're the best,'* *'Nobody can touch you,'* *'You're the next superstar.'* This sort of praise suggests the child has reached the end of their learning, and it can make the child feel complacent, or worse, scared to try something new as they might fail the next time.

3. Ask intuitive, Growth Mindset-type, open questions.

Rather than ask the child if school was good or okay today, ask: *'What did you learn today?'* *'What did you struggle with today and how did you resolve it?' 'What skills or tricks did you use to get success today?'* and *'How are you going to approach school and learning tomorrow?'*

4. Encourage children with intrinsic rewards, not extrinsic.

Never try and bribe or reward children with physical or experiential extrinsic rewards. The journey of learning should be enough in itself, especially if you fuel their aspirations for the future by having goals. Use their current progress and success to remind them they are getting closer to their goals. This intrinsic focus is where long-term gains and attitudes to learning and life are made.

Summing up Dweck's approach to Growth Mindset is her philosophy that we can do anything, but success might not be right now, it may well take some time. She uses the phrase 'not yet' when describing this process which encourages a person to keep adopting all the Growth Mindset principles above until success is achieved.

Alternatively, you might prefer to use my expression, 'success, just not yet' as opposed to speaking about failure and failing.

Mary Cai Ricci Knows Her Classroom

Backing up these experiments, but with evidence from the classroom, Mary Cai Ricci (2013) looked at children's attitudes to learning and how this was also affected by teacher expectations and possibly parents' expectations.

Between the ages of four to six, almost one hundred per cent of children exhibited a Growth Mindset, i.e. they were willing to try, to work hard, to fail, they didn't worry about negative peer feedback, etc. However, as the children started to grow up and pass through their primary education, more and more children were adopting a Fixed Mindset to learning. By the ages of eight to nine, only fifty-eight per cent of the children possessed a Growth Mindset (forty-two per cent Fixed Mindset) and by age eleven, only ten per cent of children had a Growth Mindset (ninety per cent Fixed Mindset).

For the last few years of primary education, the majority of children had started to question their own Growth Mindset. Instead of thinking, *I can do this,* many children thought, *What if I fail? What will others think? If I put in extra effort it shows I am not naturally clever.*

Many were scared to fail, often telling lies about scores on what they had learnt just to save face with their peers. In essence, the children had already decided, consciously or subconsciously, what they could do or not do and what were their strengths or weaknesses.

I feel the same is generally true for adults. We set our stall out according to our perceived skills and abilities, based on past experiences, personal, academic or professional. Often, there is a subconscious internal bias that we operate with as we approach skills, careers, people, and even performance.

The one limiting factor I have witnessed time and time again is either a lack of goals or unrealistic goals. I believe we must have goals in life and these goals once identified, will probably change over time, which is fine. However, without goals, we may be prone to navigate aimlessly through life, perhaps abandoning dreams at the first or second hurdle when we encounter a challenge.

Equally, possessing unrealistic goals, could be self-defeating. It may make us vulnerable to failures which in the short term may fire us up, but over time, can deflate us. I have seen this in education where inflated target grades are given to some pupils, and it simply acts as a demotivating factor. Even in adult professional life, being given unrealistic sales targets, for example, can demotivate people, and can create a lack of buy-in.

So, as an adult, do you try and adopt, or even adapt, some of the Growth Mindset principles and practices?

It may be that this approach will help you develop a sense of belief and therefore achievement over time.

Challenge

I like the attitude of Dweck to learning and learners. However, over the years, I have started to see things slightly differently, especially from a practical applied point of view. Having worked in over 1,500 schools, colleges and universities, I generally see what *is* and is *not* working.

According to Dweck, we should not use extrinsic rewards. This generally works with highly motivated, goal-orientated learners. However, others maybe cannot see or do not know the bigger picture to life, do not have a goal or need immediate gratification, such as a tangible reward. That could be in terms of something to own, eat/drink, getting time off, or even getting a better place in the lunchtime queue.

Rewards in themselves are a very difficult, contentious area, but for some learners, this might be the only way to engage them in Growth Mindset activity.

Similarly, if we keep saying 'not yet' without clearly explaining how to get more success, then this wears thin after a while, maybe even after a few minutes with some learners. Try using 'success, just not yet' instead. Rather, be explicit with how you get from A to B, and be patient.

As adults though, I also believe that we are not wholly and exclusively either Growth or Fixed Mindset. We can flick between the two based on motivation and expediency. This is not a bad thing, just as long as you're aware of this switch and don't keep in the Fixed Mindset zone for too long!

Many times I have witnessed high-flying corporate leaders just wanting to get a job done in an expedient way so they can focus on another challenge – I have no problem with this, just as long as it doesn't become a habit.

I Take my Hattie Off to Academic Giant, John

World-renowned academic, John Hattie (2007) is very good at distilling key learning nuggets from very complex academic research. Around these areas of developing identity, belonging, accreditation and self-worth, he talks about the value of having known support in the classroom:

"If you want to increase student academic achievement, give each student a friend."

This gives the student the sense of acceptance and connection. When all these components are in place, progress is really possible.

The power of support from friends, family and role models is powerful. It builds up our sense of identity and acceptance, and gives us a platform to receive accreditation, whether that is in childhood or adult life. Humans need acceptance, identity and belonging and when we receive compliments, along with positive and constructive feedback, we feel accredited and maybe elevated.

At the heart of this process is self-worth. We must keep believing in ourselves, learning from our 'failures' whilst persisting in the development of our skills, talents and abilities. To do this we need to recognise our own and others' Qualities and Achievements. This fuels our sense of self-worth. Giving and receiving compliments creates a win-win scenario. Even constructive feedback can act as a stepping stone to greater development opportunities.

Practically, capture your own Qualities and Achievements regularly to remind yourself of all your successes. Include everything, except anything that refers to appearance. But conversely, sharing negative and critical comments can stop others reaching their potential.

Use Post-it notes, Qualities and Achievements walls (writing down all your Q&A's) and shields (writing down your dominant Q&A's). More information is held in Lesson 2 on Confidence Development.

In Situ Accreditation – Underlay Hall Experience

Often I have witnessed cases where children are searching for accreditation. They want to prove they can do something and that they are worth something. We need to facilitate this need, be that in mainstream, special needs or in emotional behavioural difficulty children.

I encountered an example of this need to be accepted when I went for an interview for a teaching post at Underlay Hall in Cumbria in 2007. The school was comprised of a series of old buildings that had locks on every single door, almost like a prison, and housed children with extreme social, emotional and educational needs. I was being given a tour of the school by the Head and entered a number of lessons.

At first it was difficult to discern how these children had different needs to others as they all seemed to be learning and were very polite, but almost too quiet. Then a tall gentlemen in a smart jacket and tie approached me and said:

"Grand day isn't it. Is our Head looking after you?" he enquired.

"Yes he is, and it's been fascinating so far, sir," I replied.

He was the epitome of courtesy. I asked the Head about this polite staff member, and he replied:

"That's Jonny, he's one of our students. He wants to be a teacher one day and likes to pretend he's one now, like he is in practice mode. It builds up his self-worth if we just accept him… exactly like you just did."

I mentioned to the Head that it felt like a regular mainstream school. He replied that these children may present, some of the time, as quite 'normal' but there is a reason they are here, and that is because at some point they will break down, be that tears, self-isolation, destructive behaviours or pure anger and rage.

(?) *Have you ever demonstrated the need to be accredited?*

Famous Example of Accreditation – Smash it Like Martina: Game, Set & Match Acceptance

A sporting example of acceptance and accreditation, linked to identity and belonging, is that of tennis player Martina Navratilova who was born in communist Czechoslovakia and emigrated to live in America. However, the American public did not seem to endear themselves to her and she felt like an outsider.

Maybe it was her communist origins, or even her aggressive and athletic playing style that fans could not equate to female tennis. Maybe it was her outing as LGBTQ+ at a time when same sex relationships were actively frowned upon, that made her somewhat of a pariah. Even when she started to win tennis championships, she would often still feel like an outsider.

A month after her public revelation of her sexuality, at the 1981 US Open Championships, things changed forever. Even though she lost to popular American, Tracy Austin, Navratilova received a huge ovation from the crowd which made her truly emotional. In defeat, she felt she had started to be accepted by Americans. This was the turning point (BBC Gods of Tennis, 2023).

Even after 1981, her acceptance was further questioned

as she encountered some American media bias against her because she had an on-court rivalry with American sweetheart Chris Lloyd (née Evert, 1979). Rather than play into this rivalry, she rose above it to win over the media again.

She achieved this by developing her game in terms of finding marginal gains in training, performance strategy, psychological support and injury prevention. This more professional, maybe Growth Mindset approach to tennis, kept her endeared to America and the wider tennis public. It also allowed her to sustain her place as World No.1 for several years.

It is no coincidence that after she felt accepted, she went on to dominate the women's game. Before losing to Tracy Austin in 1981, she had won just two Grand Slam Singles Tournaments, but, following her defeat, she went on to win another sixteen Grand Slam Singles Titles in her illustrious career. Including Doubles and Mixed Doubles, she achieved fifty-nine Grand Slam Titles in total.

Shania is Not on the Wain

Similarly in music, singing legend, Shania Twain, has a whole host of awards and has sold over one hundred million records, making her one of the best-selling music artists of all time. Yet, she still seeks accreditation, or in her words, validation.

At Glastonbury 2024 she was being interviewed and was keen to point out that despite her success and popularity, she still needs to be validated by the Glastonbury audience; to feel she is worthy of them.

"My father gave me the greatest gift anyone could ever give another person. He believed in me." Jim Valvano (1946–1993). Former American College Basketball Player, Coach and Broadcaster. Remembered for his 1993 ESPY Awards speech while terminally ill with cancer which included his now legendary motto, *'Don't give up, don't ever give up'.*

SONOMA Waypoint Wisdom 1:

Have specific life goals and adopt daily practices to achieve these life goals.

SONOMA Waypoint Wisdom 2:

Have an appetite to prove people wrong by using perseverance and resilience, share learning, and adopt patience. These skills and qualities could help you reach your potential.

SONOMA Waypoint Wisdom 3:

Adopt a Growth Mindset throughout your whole life, i.e. believe in yourself, be prepared to put in the hard yards, do not compare, do not use or hide behind labels, enjoy a challenge and celebrate your successes.

SONOMA Waypoint Wisdom 4:

Some use of Fixed Mindset for expediency may be acceptable, but be wary of always going for the quick fix with your challenges.

SONOMA *Waypoint Wisdom* 5:

Always be open to constructive feedback – vulnerability can be a strength.

SONOMA *Waypoint Wisdom* 6:

Being accepted helps you develop your sense of identity and belonging and can lead to accreditation. Accreditation is a time when we truly arrive in life. A simple way to do this is to grow your talents and your friends.

SONOMA *Waypoint Wisdom* 7:

On your journey to accreditation never compromise either your sense of self, or your values and beliefs. Always hold your self-worth high.

SONOMA *Waypoint Wisdom* 8:

By all means develop yourself, and be proud of what you are becoming and what you stand for, but do not lose the sense of community, as no one is an island.

SONOMA *Waypoint Wisdom* 9:

Support others by being their biggest supporter. Share compliments, identify areas for improvement and build up others' sense of self-worth. Consistent support can elevate others to levels they may not have imagined, but one loose or negative comment can stay with a person for a lifetime.

QR Code Express Conversations & Mind Exercises into...
the Balance Between Growth Mindset & Fixed Mindset

Measure your performance and add scores to the PSCP Matrix at the end of the book

Personal Sonoma Colour Profile – 1: Measurements of Growth Mindset & Self-Worth

Growth Mindset Test
Answer Agree, Disagree or Sometimes

1. I think there are just some things I will not be able to improve.
2. I try to improve myself rather than compete with others.
3. When others do better than me I feel threatened.
4. I enjoy getting out of my comfort zone.
5. I can access feedback and support when necessary.
6. It is not possible to change your intelligence and abilities.
7. You should not have to try to be smart – you are smart or not.
8. I enjoy taking on new challenges or tasks with which I am unfamiliar.
9. I can give up quite easily.
10. I believe practice and sticking at something are the keys to success.

Scoring
Questions 1, 3, 6, 7, 9:
Disagree = 2 points, Sometimes = 1 point, Agree = 0 points.

Questions 2, 4, 5, 8, 10:
Agree = 2 points, Sometimes = 1 point, Disagree = 0 points.

Sonoma Gold = 16-20

You demonstrate an ability to take on challenges, have resilience, are adaptable, can access feedback and support, and are prepared to put in effort to achieve success.

Sonoma Silver = 9-15

You possess some Growth Mindset qualities, but also can drop into a Fixed Mindset of keeping to rigid preconceived ideas and practices. You have some curiosity to change but maybe need to take on a more flexible attitude to learning and life.

Sonoma Bronze = 0-8

You have some negative fixed traits that may well be holding you back. Investing in more effort, patience, asking for feedback and taking on challenges may well see you develop more of a Growth Mindset.

Self-Worth Measurement

Often our mindset is wrapped up in our self-worth, i.e. how we feel about ourselves and our achievements in life.

Below is a list of qualities. Circle the ones that mostly apply to you, i.e. are you mostly generous, mostly reliable, etc. Be honest!

Generous – Reliable – Kind – Friendly – Empathetic – Trustworthy – Good Listener – Patient – Energetic – Hard-Working – Creative – Diligent – Supportive – Attention To Detail – Organised – Responsible – Caring – Zest For Life – Optimistic – Considerate – Humble

Scoring
Each circle scores 1 point – add up your points.

Sonoma Gold = 15-21 circles
Sonoma Silver = 8-14 circles
Sonoma Bronze = 0-7 circles

P.S. If you want a really accurate measure of this, ask a friend, as peer feedback is often the most accurate.

Lesson 2:

Sow the Seeds

Leadership, Bravery, Trust, Aspiration & Confidence

Hidden Story – Ready, Steady, Go Cheese

Two mice, Ready and Steady, live with their parents in a cul-de-sac den within an underground maze of tunnels. There is only one way in and one way out to and from their den. The mice have built a barricade shutter, that once closed, makes them one hundred per cent safe from predators and they have a seemingly abundant source of cheese. Life is a little boring, but it is safe, and it is warm.

One day, Ready notices that the cheese supply is running out. He asks Steady what they should do. Steady says they should ask Mum and Dad. Mum and Dad have a chat. They decide to leave the den to find some more cheese.

After a couple of days, Mum and Dad have not returned, and the cheese supply is even lower. Ready has an idea. Instead of waiting for Mum and Dad to return, they should go and search the tunnels for more cheese. Steady starts to panic, thinking about all the negatives of this proposed action such as not finding any cheese, getting lost, being told off for not waiting for Mum and Dad or even being eaten by predators. Steady convinces Ready to stay put.

But Ready knows that action needs to be taken now. Ready decides to be brave and leaves the security of the den. He is willing to trust in fate, hoping other supplies of cheese could be found in another tunnel. Before Ready leaves, he writes a message for Steady on the den wall that reads:

What would you do if you were not afraid?

Ready is nervous, but he has made his decision. On leaving the den, he comes across a labyrinth of tunnels, an unknown network which he has never explored before. He is daunted by what he might find in terms of predators, or not finding any cheese. He explores tunnel after tunnel, and each time he leaves a tunnel he marks it with a number in the hope he can retrace his steps back to the den.

After several hours of searching, he strikes gold. He has entered a tunnel that is full of fresh cheese. He sits down and stuffs his face. He loads up with cheese and rushes home to share it with Steady.

Another day passes, and the mice are feeling hungry again. They are worried about finding more cheese, and worried about Mum and Dad. Ready decides to be brave again and leaves the den. Steady did not want to leave, trusting Mum and Dad would turn up, or even that Ready would bring back more cheese. Before he went, Ready left another message on the wall:

If you can't be brave and trust there is more cheese elsewhere, you will die.

Ready speeds off down the tunnels trying to find his way back to the tunnel with the cheese. He is flying with confidence and a need to find cheese. He quickly locates the cheese tunnel, but when he goes inside, he is shocked – all the cheese has been eaten.

What does he do now? He could cry, he could go back to Steady, or he could show more courage and trust that he will once again find more cheese. He chooses to find another cheese tunnel. He keeps numbering the tunnels and does not let panic overtake him.

He remembers what his dad once told him:

"Be brave and trust everything will work out."

With this reassuring thought in mind, he strangely starts to enjoy the challenge of finding more cheese.

Scurrying along, he stumbles across tunnel fifty-one, a goldmine of cheese – the biggest store he has ever seen in his whole life. Then Ready has a thought. Instead of relying on this one source of cheese, he will keep exploring and numbering new tunnels to locate reserve stores. He starts to find new cheese tunnels, and this gives him satisfaction and security. His courage and trust have paid off.

(Adapted from Dr Spencer, 1999).

Are there situations in your life where, with a little more trust and bravery, and a little less fear, the outcome might have been different, or even better?

As humans, I believe we must try and seek opportunities

to grow, maybe not 24/7, but that thought of growth and challenge should register and resonate within us. Rather than see every situation as a potential threat, explore the idea that a potential temporary hardship could also yield potential growth. You will know when you have achieved this mindset, when you start to enjoy and relish different challenging situations… although this attitude may not happen all the time!

Global Story – Terry Outfoxes Cancer

In 1984 when I arrived in Thunder Bay, Ontario, Canada, to study for my Master's degree in Coaching, I came across a Canadian Legend – his name was Terry Fox.

On April 20th, 1980, Terry Fox, aged twenty-one, started his Marathon of Hope journey running five thousand miles across Canada, from St John's, Newfoundland in the east, to Vancouver, British Columbia in the west. What made this feat more remarkable was that Terry Fox had a prosthetic leg, having succumbed to cancer and amputation aged just eighteen in 1977. It was this experience and seeing how people, even younger than himself, were fighting cancer that made him determined to raise funds and awareness of cancer.

The aim of the Marathon of Hope was to raise one million dollars for cancer research. This target was adjusted to twenty-four million dollars after one million dollars was reached very early (one dollar from each of the twenty-four million Canadians).

At first, there was very little publicity and only a handful of people following him. Terry would run a marathon of twenty-six miles every single day. He would get up at 4am to run twelve miles, then rest and do publicity, before running another fourteen miles in the afternoon.

Very quickly, Canadian people recognised his bravery, determination and aspiration to succeed. Along the journey he met politicians, businesspeople and athletes to raise awareness. He even stopped off to meet children with cancer. His progress was relentless, running a marathon every single day for one hundred and forty-three days (with the exception of four days rest).

On September 1st, 1980, as he approached Thunder Bay, Ontario, he had run 3,339 miles. It was at this point that Terry asked to be taken to hospital. On his stretcher he spoke to the media:

"...If there's any way I can get out there again and finish it, then I will."

Soon afterwards it was discovered that his cancer had spread to his lungs. He returned home to Port Coquitlam in British Columbia. On June 28th, 1981, Terry Fox passed away. (https://terryfox.org/terrys-story/)

To date, The Terry Fox Foundation has raised nine hundred million dollars for cancer research (Terry Fox Foundation).

This story resonates so much with me as he demonstrated unbelievable bravery, aspiring to complete a courageous run that would eventually take his life. I studied at Lakehead University in Thunder Bay (1984–86) and, in 1985, I suffered a knee and ankle injury playing in the indoor soccer leagues. These injuries and surgeries would ultimately disable me. But, unlike Terry, I can still share his story as I have done with over twenty-thousand schoolchildren to date.

I have visited his Thunder Bay statue that looks out over Lake Superior, and his statue in his hometown of Port Coquitlam in British Columbia. While I was there, I used the visit for quiet reflection and remembering quotes from Terry, to re-enthuse me on my journey. One such quote is:

"I do have a belief in God, and no matter what happens to me, things are gonna be okay. It doesn't matter whether the tumours have spread or not, because either way, I'm gonna turn out a winner."

My Story – Posting First Class Male in the Letterbox

In 1981 I started my undergraduate degree at the Carnegie School of Physical Education in Leeds. We had barely been on the course a month when we were whisked away to Buckden House in the beautiful Wharfedale Valley in the Yorkshire Dales, for a week of outdoor activities.

With a three-year degree course ahead of us, this week was clearly intended to bond and bind us together, to build confidence and trust, to develop friendships, to learn new skills, to uncover leadership traits, to test our stamina, and challenge our mental resolve. The staff also lined up a number of daring feats that would fray our nerves!

We did not know it at the time, but with trust comes bravery, and we were going to fully demonstrate both qualities. Laid out for us was an assault course that all physical education (PE) students thrived on as it provided the ideal platform to challenge ourselves physically and be competitive.

In the proceeding hour I learnt so much about myself and my 'trusted' partner. I was first to be blindfolded and while I was not totally freaked out, I was a little reserved as was often my manner at that age. With fifteen groups competing, it was very competitive and very loud. Early on in the race I bumped into a pole and then a fellow competitor.

Both incidents slowed me down as I cautiously started to think of the next collision. My stamina was slipping away, and I was worried, on the emotional verge of self-preservation rather than thinking about the glory of winning. I had lost all trust in my friend and my panic was rising.

Eventually I crossed the line thirteen out of fifteen. I was safe, but I was not covered in any glory. I realised I did not like that feeling of not giving one hundred per cent especially when unfavourable peer comments cascaded down on me afterwards. My fear of getting injured was unfounded. I made a pledge to myself that whatever other tasks were thrown at me in the next week, I was not going to feel like this again. I would trust myself and trust my partner or team.

When we reversed roles, and I supported my friend, he flew over the course, finishing second. He was certainly braver than me, had learnt a little of the course with me blindfolded and was aware that nobody had got seriously hurt. My partner trusted me more than I trusted him as there was very little hesitancy after he received my instructions.

Interestingly, the times for completion on the second run as a group were so much faster than the first run. In debriefs afterwards, a number of factors were pointed out to us:

1. When we are unsure of an initial task and outcome, we hold back.
2. When we imagine there could be physical pain, we hold back.
3. When we start to develop doubt in our heads, we hold back.
4. When we start to lose trust in our partners, we hold back.

On Day Two the stakes were raised. We were going rock climbing and caving. Just at the mere mention of this, many students started to panic, or tried to appear strong by laughing off the situation.

'Tiny' Teresa, the javelin thrower, was first to abseil down a cliff and she had a plan. She kept talking to everyone, distracting herself from the impending task. She had known for a while that when she started to overthink, things went bad, like when she overanalysed her javelin throws in competition. When the instructor said, "Teresa, you're next," she had already launched herself off the cliff before he had finished his sentence!

That was a seminal moment for her, and it was an experience she had used to help her in many similar situations in her athletic career, i.e. get talking, get distracted and do not overthink.

In the afternoon, we were to be tested again when we

got ready to go caving. Being one of the bigger students, my anxiety started to increase when I saw the narrowness of the cave tunnels. However, I just kept my head down and followed the lead instructor, trusting everything they said and asked.

Everything was going okay, and some people started to sing. As is often the case, when you face danger and realise it is not as bad as you first thought, you start to relax and enjoy the situation. Then we approached the infamous Letterbox – a rectangular slit in the rock face that resembled a tiny letterbox that we had to be 'posted' through.

I watched as others, much smaller than 'Tiny' Teresa, slipped through effortlessly. Then it was the turn of Big Billie, the county shot-putter, who rivalled 'Tiny' Teresa in size and strength. Billie confidently pushed herself through, but quickly got stuck. Instead of panicking, she sighed and cracked a joke:

"What do you call a letter that won't go through the letterbox… a big fat bill," said Billie, making fun of her larger frame. Everyone laughed, even those who were feeling scared. It broke the ice for the whole group.

She then shouted to the guy behind her to release her waistband, and asked the person who had gone through the Letterbox before her, to pull her through as she exhaled to make herself marginally slimmer. It worked, and she was posted through. The 'bill' had arrived!

The last to go was Carl, the lad from Yorkshire who was an avid caver and rock climber. He would show us how it was done, or so we thought. No sooner had he started to post himself, he had become lodged and the more he moved, the tighter lodged in he became. Carl started to have a panic attack.

Out of the darkness came the calm voice of 'Tiny' Teresa: "Now, Carl, remember, fear is a choice. Just remember that and relax by breathing slowly and we will do the rest." Carl did as he was told, and he was duly posted.

I know these examples are not anything like those SAS-style situations, but at that age of development, we had conquered some fears and had learnt how we operated best when we were tested. These experiences would stand us in good stead for future years.

The biggest lesson I took away from the week was that if you let your fear overtake your rational thinking, you will soon become nervous of every single situation that you encounter. Not only will you feel nervous, but you will not be able to give your best. This is a classic definition of underperformance. Sadly, some people spend a lifetime in this state. Back yourself, and trust in your team and it may well take you a very long way in life.

Have you ever been in a situation where you backed yourself and you eventually came through?

Have you ever been in a situation where you did not back yourself and you struggled?

Deep Dive – Bravery – I'm A Celebrity... Get Me in Here!

If we are to be brave, we might need some training to dial us in, so that when we face that fear, we can react in an automatic or subconscious way, rather than panic. This instinctive capability is apparent with military personnel in war zones, the paramedics attending horrendous incidents and mental health first aider (MHFA) people when they are thrust into saving someone who is suicidal.

Sometimes people become brave when there is no other choice, or a 'tipping point' occurs in life when there is no going back.

Through life's experiences you may well develop bravery and it may serve you well. These experiences can also be manufactured, as was the case within television reality shows such as *I'm A Celebrity… Get Me Out Of Here!* during which celebrities attempt daring challenges. On the 2022 show, comedian Babatunde Aleshe, newsreader Charlene White and former England footballer Jill Scott had to walk out onto a plank suspended one hundred and fifty feet high on the roof of a building while being held in a safety harness.

Charlene White managed to walk slowly and nervously the few yards to the end of the plank, just about overcoming her fear with support from Jill. However, Babatunde Aleshe let his fears overcome him and could not complete the task. Jill Scott sprinted to the end of the plank, overriding or disrespecting the potential fear of death.

How did she do this?

Maybe she saw the goal of winning a challenge was greater than letting fear control her? Or did she think of the kudos she would receive for her post-football career within the media?

Whatever the reasons, she overcame fear by adopting a rational choice to her situation rather than letting fear take control. Maybe James Haskell was right when he said that *fear is a choice*, which I think he pinched off 'Tiny' Teresa.

Homegrown Bravery

It is relevant, appropriate and wholly necessary to include a note about someone who demonstrates bravery and courage every single day. He is an international speaker, trainer and ex-professional footballer.

For many years he has been in high demand across the globe from high-performing business organisations as they seek his counsel. But in recent years he has been facing his own health challenges which have dictated that he steps back from the business world.

What I have noticed about him is that he deals with this health challenge as he would a business challenge. He looks at things logically, accepts what he can and can't do, and is optimistic – qualities that only a few could possibly aspire to.

His name is Mel Tottoh, and I am proud to call him a friend, a mentor and a brother.

Deep Dive – Trust – The True Professionals

In life, we may well have to trust others and trust the process within areas such as business, medicine, education, sports, and relationships for example. We trust doctors and surgeons, sometimes with our lives. A blind person trusts their guide dog. We trust the airline pilot when we board the plane. Maybe it is because often, when we encounter these professionals, we have little choice. Clearly, if you have experienced a plane crash, a poor operation outcome, or your guide dog has led you into a lamp-post, this trust will have been shaken!

Over the years you may have learnt to yield and trust more in people and processes. If this has been the case, I suspect your progress will have improved when you have adopted this viewpoint. We can spend a lifetime worrying, but it serves no real purpose. In fact, as we age, worrying can not only create procrastination, and lost opportunities, but it can fuel disease within our bodies (Lesson 9).

Deep Dive – Leadership – Curiously Following Colin Powell Anywhere

Colin Powell was a decorated soldier and once held the highest USA military post of Chairman of the Joint Chiefs of Staff. He had a career that saw him involved in twenty-eight military crises and was considered an experienced safe pair of hands for global conflicts. Following his distinguished military career, he used his experiences to become an accomplished public speaker, often talking about leadership and trust. The following quote succinctly sums up this approach:

> *"Good leaders are people who are trusted by followers. To be trusted you must prepare your men, you must demonstrate to your men, and you must serve them selflessly. When you're cold, tired, hungry and terrified, you can't show your men you're cold, tired, hungry and terrified. When a leader has*

developed good trust, his men will follow him, if only out of curiosity." (YouTube, 2011).

I think if he had included women in that statement, it might have been even more impactful!

Tim Does not Cook The Books at Apple

Many people will know of Steve Jobs as the face of Apple. He was the hugely successful CEO who made Apple a global brand. But up until his death in 2011, his autocratic leadership skills, according to various sources, left much to be desired, with reports of bad behaviour and an over-controlling nature (*Psychology Today*, 2012).

Taking over the helm of Apple in 2011 was Tim Cook who has a distinctive and effective leadership style. He begins sending emails at 4.30am each weekday and has Sunday night staff meetings by telephone to prepare for the following week. His leadership focuses on people, strategy, and execution, stating that, "If you get those three right, the world is a great place."

Beyond these three elements, and his unique meeting arrangements, he likes to be more hands off, a more macro-management approach within a collaborative culture, which contrasts with Steve Jobs who practised micro-management and issued controlling instructions.

Cook has tripled Apple's revenue, adding billions to the bottom line. He is also putting the environment, privacy, inclusivity and diversity at the forefront of the company's values. He has grown donations to charity and is committed to energy renewables (Wikipedia, Tim Cook).

Far be it for me to contradict such a successful businessperson, but would you like reminder emails at 4.30am each weekday and a telephone meeting that severely hits into your private social time?

Simon Sinek is Surprised in a Hotel!

A world-renowned speaker, author and social commentator is Simon Sinek. He recounts a story of a hotel worker who experiences two different styles of leadership and reacts differently to both (YouTube, 2021).

As he entered the first hotel, the Four Seasons, he came across an engaging and friendly barista called Noah. They chatted politely. During the course of the conversation, Noah told him how happy he was at the Four Seasons, how he looked forward to coming to work and if he were ever asked to do extra work or run errands, he would do it without any hesitation. His managers would often stop him and ask if they could do anything to help him do his own job better.

Noah then added that he also worked at Caesars Palace Hotel which he did not like, as his managers, rather than asking him what they could do for him to execute his job better, were looking for ways in which they could catch him out!

Which sort of leader or manager are you?

Deep Dive – Aspiration – RAS is Switched on to Find What You Want

In terms of aspiration, the ability and desire to achieve, have goals, and reach above your current situation is a laudable quality, which is often missing in those who are 'happy with their lot'. Indeed, being optimistic and aspirational, may well alter our chemical profile for the better. For example, we know that the production of negative hormones such as Cortisol can be suppressed if we are happier.

The production of the reward hormone Dopamine makes us feel upbeat and optimistic about achieving something. Equally, when we are happier in our emotional minds, this can have a positive impact on our physical health, like a symbiotic relationship, where one feeds the other. How we think can affect the physiological functioning of our bodies.

There is also a part of the brain called the reticular activating system (RAS) that is located in the brain stem and hypothalamus. If stimulated with consistent positive, aspirational thoughts, even images, it can start to subconsciously seek out these aspirations in real life.

In terms of the RAS, once it consistently receives a positive or wanted image, it starts to search for it. For example, if I said you have ten thousand pounds and you have to spend it on a BMW car, your RAS will make you aware of BMW cars, and you are now more alert to looking for more types of the BMW car range.

The theory to this thinking is the same as when we use positive affirmations – we start to see the positive results in daily life. Aspiration on the whole is a very positive attribute and one that many successful people possess and often demonstrate throughout their whole lives.

The only caveat could be when we become consistently overly aspirational, almost obsessional, when aspiration overrides all other emotions. This might deliver results, but it could also bring unwanted outcomes such as a loss of friends and colleagues, and it may invite poor health. A smart professional will intuitively know when aspiration is serving a purpose and when it is becoming counter-productive.

Aspiration may be closely aligned to optimism and when we are more optimistic this has many benefits for us as humans as you will find out in Lesson 10.

Are you aware when you are at this overly aspirational tipping point?

Deep Dive – Confidence – Quick & Longer-Term Wins

There is another component that binds together bravery, trust, aspiration and leadership, and it is also fundamental to each component. This component is confidence, which in simple terms, is not being scared to think, say or act.

Outwardly, confidence is the ability to have a strong self-belief, an appetite to speak in public, being able to volunteer when others do not want to or simply being quiet without feeling intimidated. It also manifests itself when allowing others to speak and share opinions. Confidence can be detected when developing skills, abilities, and qualities without fear of reprisal or rejection, having the curiosity to attempt new activities, not having the need for external validation… and the list goes on.

A phrase which sums up confidence is:

"Confidence is not 'Will they like me?'. Confidence instead is 'I'll be fine if they don't'."

Without confidence, it may well be impossible to develop these other Lesson 2 components, and indeed, develop virtually every other component in the Twelve Lessons. But confidence can only be developed once we have a foundation of self-worth – it sits above it, like the canopy of an umbrella locked into the handle for support. When a strong and robust handle is in place (self-worth), then the canopy of the umbrella can be opened (confidence).

Given its importance, how can we develop and grow it to last a lifetime? How do we get the 'canopy of confidence' to open, and stay open?

If you google 'confidence' in 2024, you will uncover nearly three million hits. There is an overabundance of short talks on the internet such as Ted Talks on confidence, ranging from enlightening to damaging. In short, accessing valid confidence development is a minefield.

We are all born with the same amount of confidence potential, but it is our journey and interpretations through life, especially in our formative years, that can dictate our confidence outcomes. Humans have some six thousand thoughts a day and seventy-five per cent of these can be negative. We are designed this way to survive, but we can be too focused on this outcome. This genetic predisposition to negativity may be a root cause for a lack of confidence in some people.

Supportive parents or carers, teachers, employers and even celebrities are crucial. These role models set out the template for confidence development, whether they know it or not. It is about reinforcing confident behaviour, modelling self-confident behaviour, creating an environment where there is no pressure or expectation, but a curiosity to experience, learn, develop and even fail.

Confidence is further developed if these same role models consistently believe in us, provide us with opportunities and communicate our progress. Confidence often flows when we have a passion or niche knowledge about something. Our fear of performance can be relegated when we are in this flow of passion. Confidence must be continually worked on and cannot be ring-fenced once you have it. When we stop demonstrating confident behaviours we may lose some aspects of confident performance.

Sometimes we just need more or better preparation, guidance, and practice to overcome a temporary failure. This is when confidence links with resilience. Try and learn where it went wrong. We often learn more from our failures than our successes.

You may already have confidence without knowing it. On your own, or with trusted others, why don't you take a retro journey to rediscover historical confident demonstrations around thoughts, feelings and actions.

Confidence can be grown and developed. Parents, grandparents, siblings, carers, friends, colleagues, celebrities and those educating or employing us can be pivotal to this development. Choose these people carefully if you can. Fortunately or unfortunately, you can't choose your family!

What I have witnessed though, is that when we encounter setbacks and are triumphant, our confidence is enhanced. For me, the ability to overcome setbacks is the mark of a truly confident person. This bounce-back confidence is symbiotically linked to resilience (more about resilience in Lesson 5).

Challenge

How do we distil out the key constituents and actions needed that also takes into account individual differences? What might be good development tips for one person, might be extremely harmful for another. This is where bespoke coaching, coaxing, and fully understanding a person is crucial.

In Situ Confidence – The Girl At Ripley St Thomas Has Confidence

One of my many school teaching experiences was at Ripley St Thomas School in Lancaster. I did not know much about the school, other than it was a school that had high standards of behaviour and performance. However, often I have found that this can lead to children being a little too cheeky and familiar, almost devious at times. So, as I entered this Year 9 class to deliver French, I was on my guard.

I started off by standing up to assert a physical presence, and told the class of my expectations, and what I would not tolerate. I suppose I was going on a little, but I have found that this approach usually works for me.

Then a girl puts her hand up, and asks a question:

"Can we start now please?"

This was a reminder that not only was she confident enough to confront this strange giant in her classroom in front of her peers, but she was also eager to learn. A classic case of not being bothered or scared about others or even myself – she had confidence.

Have you ever had this type of confidence when you have gone against the flow of opinion or expectation?

Bonus Story – My Tipping Point – No Bald Head Then

Sometimes we can use the fear of failure to spur us on to develop confidence. I call this a 'tipping point' and my first was my failed examinations, and then my acne was second, both of which made me feel inferior and therefore less confident. I have since used these experiences to prove organisations and people wrong about me and it can be a strong driving force which has catapulted me into confident behaviours and emotions.

My public speaking tipping point happened when I was at Carnegie College, I was twenty years old. Along with the rest of my cohort, we had to present a Wednesday lecturette of ten minutes to our peers. This filled me with dread, so much so that for several weeks I pretended to be ill. Strangely enough I was only ever ill on Wednesdays, and always on the morning of the lecturette.

I eventually summoned up enough courage to deliver my presentation. All I can say is that it went by without me turning into a gibbering wreck, but equally, it was not a great performance as I had my head down, staring at my notes, and talking like a fast robot. It was this singular experience that made me make a promise to myself – to never be intimidated by others when public speaking again.

I would not employ this head down non-engagement of the audience now, if only for one reason – nobody would be able to concentrate on my speech as they would be distracted by my bald head! Barring a few small hiccups in my twenties, I have enjoyed speaking in public for the past thirty years.

Is your lack of confidence stopping you from enjoying public speaking?

Famous Example of Bravery & Belief – Mark Beaumont Rides & Rows Again

In 2009, I bumped into a chap waiting for an elevator in Salt Lake City, Utah. What made this impromptu meeting strange were two things. The first was that I had just had some drastic facial laser surgery with Dr Mark Taylor, and I was not a pretty sight. At six feet two inches and eighteen stone, with small streams of blood running down my face and an overall redness that could have matched Mars, I resembled a blushing Elephant Man.

Secondly, this chap was not intimidated at all. In fact, he was curious. He happily chatted about my face. Then I asked him what he was doing in Salt Lake City. He talked modestly about cycling solo down the coast from Alaska to Argentina. As we chatted away for a couple of minutes, I realised that this guy was a bit special.

He said he had to get to bed for a few hours as he was on his bike again tomorrow, around 3am. He gave me his social media tour details so we could stay connected. He was intrigued to find out if the surgery had been a success.

I did not know it at the time, but he was a world record breaking endurance athlete, and broadcaster. It was Mark Beaumont, and he has many successes and a few failures:

- Rode solo from John o'Groats to Land's End aged fifteen in 1998.
- Broke the Guinness World Record for circumnavigating the world on a bicycle in 2008.
- Cycled from Alaska to Southern Argentina for a 2010 BBC TV series.
- Rowed across Canada in 2011.
- Failed to row across the Atlantic from Morocco to Barbados in 2012.
- Holds the record of fastest solo cycle along the length of Africa in forty-two days in 2015.
- In 2017 he obtained the world record for cycling around the world (in seventy-nine days).

Often, giants of athletic feats are not so well known outside their immediate worlds. They do not have the full celebrity status, but nevertheless, their feats and whole manner are truly breathtaking.

Mark Beaumont was assured, very brave and aspirational, but he also has immense self-belief. Yet, he did not overplay his hand, being modest and confident in equal, well-balanced measures. Without doubt, his endurance challenges have made him what he is today.

Even in our communications for this book, he was engaging, humble and was keen to assist in any way he could.

"The best way to find out if you can trust somebody is to trust them." Ernest Hemingway (1889–1961) – American writer, ambulance driver in WWI, and journalist who won the Nobel Prize for Literature in 1954.

SONOMA Waypoint Wisdom 10:

Sometimes fear is overcome with the support of others, a pure necessity of circumstance or even to prove someone wrong.

SONOMA Waypoint Wisdom 11:

We often do not know how brave we are, until we have to face a challenge. The challenge can instil within us a sense of courage and bravery that we didn't think we possessed, and the outcomes can be beautiful and could maybe last a lifetime.

SONOMA Waypoint Wisdom 12:

In life, for whatever reason, we may set our perceived limits lower than our capacity because of fear. Over time, this may give way to underachievement and discontentment. Be wary of this condition by remembering that maybe fear is a choice?

SONOMA Waypoint Wisdom 13:

Trust in yourself and trust in the future, and you might surprise yourself with how much progress you start to make in the present.

SONOMA Waypoint Wisdom 14:

Some leaders can be empowering while others can demoralise employees. Good leaders may instil curiosity while others may be too didactic. Ensure your leadership style incorporates empowerment, curiosity and maybe a blend of micro-management (hands on) and macro-management (hands off).

SONOMA Waypoint Wisdom 15:

Aspiration can breed optimism and our brains thrive off this Dopamine-based emotion. However, being too aspirational may possibly be counter-productive. As we travel through life, our aspirations may change according to our needs.

SONOMA Waypoint Wisdom 16:

A supportive 'tribe' of friends and colleagues who reflect back your qualities and achievements, and offer constructive feedback are very powerful contributors to confidence development. Choose and use your friends wisely.

SONOMA Waypoint Wisdom 17:

Do not compare yourself to anyone else. Yes, have role models but do not compete against them or anyone else. You are on your own path.

SONOMA Waypoint Wisdom 18:

Try and develop a skill, talent or ability. When we do this we often have to practise, and refine, maybe work with others and take guidance. Ultimately, when we make our breakthrough it can make us feel accredited by others. Accreditation fuels confidence.

SONOMA Waypoint Wisdom 19:

Support others on their confidence journeys, i.e. do not pull the ladder up from behind you, rather extend the ladder or offer a helping hand to others. Celebrate together. Confident people grow confidence in others.

SONOMA Waypoint Wisdom 20:

When we face setbacks and recover or bounce back, our confidence can be enhanced, and this is a solid platform to build resilience. Remember, 'often the darkest part of the night is followed by the dawn of the light'.

SONOMA Waypoint Wisdom 21:

Do not fall into the trap of self-sabotage. Reflect back on behaviours, emotions and opinions, but be careful not to do this with a negative filter. Review performance starting with a positive filter, and then review outcomes with trusted others.

QR Code Express Conversations & Mind Exercises into...
Developing Confidence & Building Trust

Measure your performance and add scores to the PSCP Matrix at the end of the book

Personal Sonoma Colour Profile –
2: Measurements of Confidence & Trust

Confidence Measure
Answer:
Strongly agree – Agree – Disagree – Strongly disagree

1. I see challenges as part of my everyday thoughts and activities.
2. I think doing action is important.
3. I enjoy searching for my talents and finding what I'm good at.
4. I don't recognise my achievements and qualities.
5. I find the positives in each situation.
6. I 'keep going' after I haven't been successful.
7. I think there can be more than one view of the same event.
8. I compare with others.
9. I see practice as a part of being successful at challenges.
10. I can't go against the tide of opinion.

Scoring
Questions 1, 2, 3, 5, 6, 7, 9:
4 Strongly agree – 3 Agree – 2 Disagree – 1 Strongly disagree.

Questions 4, 8, 10:
1 Strongly agree – 2 Agree – 3 Disagree – 4 Strongly disagree.

Sonoma Gold = 30-40
Clearly you possess confidence and are prepared to demonstrate this and even go against the flow of opinion at times. You have self-assurance and can complete tasks. However, you may have a tendency to be overconfident, even arrogant.

Sonoma Silver = 16-29
Good levels of confidence exist but you may be prone to dwelling on perceived failures for too long. If you are prepared to take on new challenges or complete old ones, your rating will soar.

Sonoma Bronze = 1-15
Displays of confidence are inconsistent and you may think about what will go wrong rather than what can go right? You have plenty of room for improvement if you can be brave and patient.

Trust Measure
Below are six key trust components. Do you have all six?
1. Being reliable.
2. Seeing things through by delivering on promises.
3. Transparent in decision-making and motivation.
4. Listen to the input of others.
5. Put the interest of others over all else when appropriate.
6. Confidence and belief.

If you want to measure trust further, according to Charles H Green & Andrea Howe (2011), then you must consistently display the following characteristics of Credibility,

Reliability, Intimacy and Self-Orientation.

Here is an adapted quick test to see if you possess trust.

Answer Yes or No

1. Credibility
- Do you have a good level of professional knowledge?
- Do you have a good level of professional skill?
- Do you have a good level of professional experience?
- Are you perceived as an expert in your field?
- When you give information, do people trust you that it's accurate and up to date?
- Outside of your professional life, would people say you are trustworthy?

2. Reliability
- Do you do what you say you will do?
- Are you a good timekeeper?
- Are you rarely absent?
- Do you under-promise and over-deliver?

3. Intimacy
- Do you feel secure sharing a view that is different to others?
- Do you make room for people to speak up and share ideas?
- Do you share personal details and habits?
- Are you professional yet approachable?

4. Self-Orientation

- Are you less interested in getting what you need at the expense of looking good?
- Do you genuinely care about others?
- Do you make sure you collaborate fully to achieve team goals?
- Do you rate self-interest lower than team interest?

Scoring

Each Yes scores 1 point.

Sonoma Gold = 14-18

Clearly people trust you. You have good awareness of others' needs whilst keeping to promises and deadlines. You lead by example, and this builds further trust within the organisation.

Sonoma Silver = 9-13

Good levels of trust exist between you and others. However, there is room for improvement, and you might need to demonstrate this to yourself and others. It may be a lack of consistency and transparency is having a negative impact on trust.

Sonoma Bronze = 1-8

Trust levels are low and probably inconsistent. There might need to be an overhaul of how you operate in relation to colleagues and managers... before it's too late!

Lesson 3:

Nurture & Cultivate

Adversity, Strengths, Passion & Mental Health

Hidden Story – Make Mine a Double Trouble?

Two brothers who were identical twins were raised by an abusive alcoholic father. Their father not only greatly abused alcohol, but tortured and tormented the brothers physically, verbally, and emotionally for years.

Many years later, an individual was greatly intrigued by the success of one of the brothers and sought out a chance to interview him. This individual wanted to know what this brother attributed his success to.

When asked directly, the brother replied, "I had to find a way up and out. My alcoholic father terribly abused my brother and me when we were kids. I knew that if I didn't work hard and seek a better life, I would end up just like my father."

The interviewer was amazed and began to wonder about how the other brother turned out and what he would attribute such a life to. So, the interviewer began the process of tracking him down.

The other brother was eventually found to be homeless and living in the streets as a bum. The interviewer asked, "What do you attribute your bad situation and luck to?"

This brother replied, "I had no choice. My alcoholic father terribly abused my brother and me when we were kids. I didn't stand a chance."

Challenge

This is far too simplistic an explanation for me. I have been around far too long, and have experienced many aspects of growth and development to know there is often more to dealing with adversity than it just being a simple choice.

Global Story – The Famous Five & Arnie Will be Back

There are many global stories about adversity that I could detail here. Examples could be:

- **Oprah Winfrey** experienced physical and sexual abuse from family members, was raped at age nine, became pregnant at fourteen (subsequently lost the baby). It was her father who insisted education was the way to be more than who she was.

- **Tom Cruise** grew up with an abusive father in extreme poverty. He had a late diagnosis of dyslexia which hindered his academic journey but ignited a passion within him to succeed.

- **Alvin Law** is a Canadian actor, disc jockey and musician (mastering the piano, trombone and drums). He is a victim of the thalidomide scandal that left him without arms, and was abandoned by his birth family and put up for adoption. He learnt to use his feet and toes to live independently and has shared his story with over two million people, and is a Canadian Hall of Fame inductee and a global speaker.

Other people who experienced adversity in adult life include:

- **Aron Ralston** in 2003, aged twenty-seven, got stuck behind an 800lb boulder whilst rock climbing in Utah. After one hundred and twenty-seven hours of being pinned behind the rock he decided he had to cut off his forearm to survive. He lived to become an international activist and motivational global speaker.

- **Viktor Frankl** became an MD in 1930 and was the head of the neurology department at Rothschild Hospital, Vienna in 1940. At the age of thirty-seven, he was imprisoned in a total of four Nazi concentration camps including Auschwitz and Dachau. His father, mother, brother and wife did not survive the camps. Viktor survived by looking for the positives of his situation in a humorous light – in spite of his cruel and inhumane treatment.

A very interesting story that is appropriate here, and parallels with the story above, is that of Arnold Schwarzenegger and his older brother Meinhard, and how their father's behaviour impacted both lives.

Both grew up with their abusive father who was scarred by wartime experiences (probably undiagnosed PTSD) and who was violent, depressive and experiencing schizophrenia. This experience made Arnie determined to leave his home and country of Austria in 1968 aged twenty-one to seek his destiny in bodybuilding.

He built on his strengths of natural genetic size, added motivation and a passion for knowledge to become probably the best bodybuilder the world had ever seen. Nothing was going to stop him, not even his father! It may be said that he was successful because his father was the catalyst for positive change.

However, Meinhard, scarred by this upbringing, became more distant and reclusive. He started to develop a drinking problem and had become erratic with work, people and relationships. He died in a drink-drive accident in 1971 aged twenty-five. His father was the catalyst for negative change and ultimately his life was ended early.

Arnie succinctly sums up the adversity:

"Nietzsche was right. That which doesn't kill you makes you stronger, but the very thing that made me strong today, was the very thing that destroyed Meinhard."

Again, it is often aphorisms like those espoused by Nietzsche that people hold dear and true, the world over. Yet, sadly as we have seen with Meinhard, the impact can be life-ending. There is more to dealing with adversity than just facing it up.

My Story – Challenging School Days

I started working full time with emotional behavioural difficulties (EBD) pupils from 2008–2011. For the very first time, I understood how a fractured and traumatised upbringing could have a devastating impact on a child at a young age, and often, this impact could probably last for a lifetime.

I had worked as a teacher in mainstream schools for several years, and I had worked in special educational needs (SEN) and some challenging pupil referral units (PRU's) in Preston, Blackpool and St Helens. I had encountered physical threats, and learnt how to handle children safely when things erupted. I had been threatened with knives and had witnessed extreme forms of violence.

But nothing prepared me for my three years working in Blackburn with the 'highest tariff' pupils of ages fourteen – sixteen in class sizes of only three pupils, with a mere fourteen pupils in the whole school. This was a last-chance saloon school where if we could not manage behaviours, the pupils would more than likely go to a secure unit.

These pupils, through no fault of their own, had experienced a shocking upbringing. Many had experienced physical, emotional and sexual abuse. Some had been in serious trouble with the police, and many had multiple SEN diagnoses. Sadly, many were bereft of a sense of self-worth, belonging, and positive identity. It made me wonder how children so young could have been exposed to such abuse, deprivation and utter adversity.

Every day I went into work having to teach, restrain, counsel and engage children who were struggling on all fronts. Every day somebody would be fighting, somebody would be frustrated, somebody would be giving up, somebody would be crying, somebody would not be learning, somebody would be in a restraining hold, somebody would be destroying equipment, and somebody would be absent.

Occasionally pupils would show dangerous bravery in PE or social activities to gain accreditation that they were worth something. This could involve running into walls after a ball was passed, or barging fearlessly into bigger and stronger pupils, and even staff. I now see that these were attempts to feel valued.

All the time, I was thankful to my parents for providing me with what these pupils sadly did not receive, i.e. a secure foundation of unconditional love, a safety net to make choices and see what I could achieve, a provision of a safe house and environment, a sense of belonging to a loving family and supportive community, and a real sense of self-worth which was accredited on a daily basis.

After three years, the EBD school closed, which was part of a wider school business reorganisation. I was thankful as I was almost burnt out. I was also humbled that I had tried to make a difference to the lives of those young people. Many I had taught had achieved high passes in GCSE ICT (Information Communication Technology) and beyond this, I hoped that my relaxed way of engaging with them, my corny jokes and my sense of one hundred per cent support, might have rubbed off in some small way.

What did I learn and what did I do next as a result of this experience?

I learnt that life is not fair. I experienced how and why a safe upbringing was crucial. Furthermore, if this upbringing could be mixed with unconditional love, support, and a provision of opportunities, then self-development and self-worth could be nurtured in the formative years of youth.

I also learnt that you should never give up on people or their situations. I was constantly reminded of this through various 'experiences' that surprised me in a good way. One example of this was when we were conducting a sports day for the EBD children at Witton Park in Blackburn. Along with a good compliment of support staff, we had around eight children who wanted to experience a formal athletics competition. We laid on several events such as long jump, high jump, one hundred metres, four hundred metres and relay. We decided not to hold the discus, shot and javelin events!

For the relay event, I had an official starting pistol. Two teams lined up for the relay, I fired the pistol and the children raced off. However, what I had not noticed was that a stranger had started to approach me in a menacing manner, shouting obscenities at me.

Very quickly he was in my personal space threatening me for using a pistol. It was clear that this man had his own challenges, but nevertheless he posed a threat. As I tried to reason with him, the children seemed to recognise this threat, and they ran across to me. They surrounded this man, and made it clear that nobody was going to spoil their sports day. Then, my star pupil, Jake, looked at this man and said:

"Listen, I don't care who you are, nobody is stopping

our sports day. Don't even think about giving Mr Mc any more grief or you will have us to deal with."

The words he used were delivered in a voice hardened by a short life full of trauma, distrust and anger. Yes, he meant business. I had seen that look in Jake's eyes before and physical assault was its promise, rather than a vague threat. The man turned away and started to sprint to safety. The children cheered and for a moment Jake was a hero – an instance that he had probably never experienced in his short life before.

I also learnt that without self-worth, which can be fuelled in situations like the menacing stranger on sports day, it was almost impossible to achieve any kind of sustained success, whichever way you measured that success.

When adversity is encountered at a young age, it can have a devastating lifelong impact on mental health, relationships, employability, quality of life, and life expectancy. Sometimes no amount of love, trust and support can counter the negative impacts of early years adversity.

Thankfully, there are cases where adversity is overcome. This was part of the reason I started to write my children's books which were aimed at developing self-worth, confidence and identity in children ages eight – eleven. I wanted to give parents, carers and teachers the tools to support young people, hopefully before trauma and difficult situations were encountered. Or at the very least, give them some tools to deal reactively with adversity.

Deep Dive – Adversity – There are Many Approaches

Our ability to fight adversity is dependent on our filter on the world or our Frame of Reference. Each person is slightly different in terms of age, physical shape, home and education experiences, gender, sexuality, religion, health, finances, support, aspiration, opportunity, trauma, etc. This is why it is important not to judge people, especially when they are facing adversity. You simply do not know their background and potential baggage.

For some, a 'face your demons or be damned' tactic like that adopted by Oprah, Tom, Alvin, Aron and Viktor would be appropriate given they had very little option but to fight. Indeed, this fight also made them stronger. However, for others with a different Frame of Reference, like those children I encountered at the EBD school, mounting and sustaining a successful response to adversity is probably not possible.

Dealing with adversity involves a collective response. There are examples in history when people have faced annihilation and operated as one defiant unit. The war in Ukraine has revealed videos featuring its citizens sheltering underground, waving phone lights and singing. This was their way of dealing with the adversity of war.

Have you ever faced adversity, and if so, how did you deal with it and interpret that experience afterwards?

Let's now look at strengths with a view to seeing how this component can impact our ability to develop, and fight adversity.

Deep Dive – Strengths – How Many Neurones & Synapses do You Have?

You might have heard the phrase, 'develop your strengths but always work on your weaknesses'. This has certainly been levelled at me over the years, but as I have aged, I realise that developing my strengths gives me more passion, and that fuels my quest of becoming better and reaching my potential.

For sure, I am aware of my 'areas for improvement' shall we say, but I believe I will make more gains by focusing on what I can do well, and then work to do it even better – that is where my passion lies. I am not alone in this thinking as Marcus Buckingham and Donald Clifton (2001) also align themselves to this view of strengths and passion. In fact, they have even created measurement tools to prove your strengths, when identified and polished, will gain you more progress than working on, and worrying about, your areas for improvement.

They explain this by reference to our early brain development and how this development is fuelled or stunted by strengths and passion. The growth and proliferation of brain cells (neurones) and how they connect with one another (synapses), is phenomenal.

- Day 42: first neurone is created.
- Day 120: one hundred billion neurones exist.

- After three years we have fifteen thousand synapses for each neurone of each of the one hundred billion neurones.
- As we age beyond three, nature and our own practices, start to strip out unwanted or unused neural pathways.
- We lose billions of them and by the time we wake up on our sixteenth birthday, half of our network is gone.

Nature does this to allow you to capitalise on your strongest connections, so you become more efficient. This is why many observers of human development advise you to work on your strengths rather than your weaknesses. The good news is that we can also adapt and adjust these neurones, pathways, and synapses later in life – so it is not all over at sixteen! This is called neuroplasticity.

Through my work, especially in independent schools, I have noticed how many young children are encouraged to play musical instruments. There is evidence that suggests being musical at a young age helps other parts of the brain develop, like mathematical ability (Matthew Syed, 2011). Only recently, there was a study that suggested being early years musicians could actually delay or even stave off forms of dementia in later life (Walsh, Causer & Brayne, 2019).

How does this link to challenging adversity?

So, when we encounter adversity, this neuroplasticity comes to the fore. Neuroplasticity can occur after injury as we learn new ways to walk, talk and interact with the world. It is also apparent when we develop new habits, either good or bad. These pathways can be made following a good diet and exercise regime, or in response to drug addiction, abuse, examination failure or stress. The brain cannot tell the difference between good and bad, and goes to do what it knows, and crucially, what is easiest and what is already hardwired.

Linked very closely to this concept, we have seen the work of Mary Cai Ricci who talked about developing a Growth Mindset or a Fixed Mindset, especially before ages ten and eleven.

> *Given what we now know about the brain's development after three years, should you be working with children at an even younger age?*

So, the good news is that we can change our neuroplasticity and Mindsets, and this can help us develop strengths, and good habits, but can it really help us overcome adversity, especially if we have encountered mental health challenges when we are young?

> *Does challenging adversity negatively impact our mental health – is adversity a double-edged sword?*

Deep Dive – Mental Health – We are All Different

Our mental health is significantly influenced when we are younger. According to MHFA in 2020, fifty per cent of all mental ill health happens before the age of fourteen, and seventy-five per cent before age twenty-four. So, getting into your early twenties only represents a twenty-five per cent chance of developing mental illness in later life. Equally, women between ages sixteen to twenty-four are almost three times more likely to develop a mental illness (twenty-six per cent) as compared to men (nine per cent).

People from Black and Asian backgrounds can experience more physical health-related problems such as diabetes and heart disease, as well as stigma which can contribute to poorer mental health. Similarly, people from LGBTQ+, SEN and certain cultural or religious faith backgrounds may also experience more stigma which can have an adverse impact on mental health.

Also, mental health can be impacted by those who experience physical disability, long-term pain (or exposure to non-physical forms of trauma), those who experience poorer living standards, and those who have a lack of access to vital physical and mental health services.

So, it seems we have an unfair or uneven playing field when it comes to challenging adversity. This unfairness can be magnified when we are younger as I have sadly witnessed first-hand. But poor mental health and mental ill health can also appear in later life when it can have an equally devastating impact on us, and our capacity to perform in life, and overcome adversity.

We will further cover mental health later in this lesson and with further examples of when mental health is compromised in Lesson 9 (Burn-Out, Rust-Out and general anxiety) and in Lesson 10 (response strategies).

Special Bonus Story – The Gift of Ryan

Beyond my early work with numerous groups of children who were struggling with their mental health, I have been fortunate to help bring up a young man called Ryan. I met him in 1988 when he was about twelve months old, and he is now thirty-six, and he is a beautiful part of my life. For various reasons Ryan did not have an easy upbringing.

He is enthusiastic, but possesses no formal qualifications or skills, and sometimes lives day to day looking for work. He struggles with his mental health at times, but his big heart always shines through. In my relationship with him it is important for me to take things slowly, often one small step at a time, and with plenty of encouragement and belief in him. I see my role as one of continual support and guidance. So, I will help him to pass his driving test, get some accredited skills, and one day, financially support him so he can own a house.

What makes me really proud is that he calls me Dad. I try and live up to that label and I am always there for him. I encourage him, and I believe in him.

As a result of dealing with many groups of young people with mental health challenges, I eventually became an accredited trainer with MHFA England in 2019. It has been an investment that has changed my life, and hopefully the lives of others.

Famous Example of Strengths & Passion — Don't Underestimate Wilf Paish's Stature

Wilf Paish was a British athletics coach and trained athletes like Olympic champion Tessa Sanderson, javelin thrower Mick Hill and runner Peter Elliott. If you were an athlete in the 1970s and 80s you knew about Wilf. He was one of my tutors at Carnegie School of Physical Education (1981–

84). I will never forget the first time we all met him, and he introduced himself:

"My name is Wilf Paish, spelt G. O. D."

He was a man of short stature, but was an athletics giant who certainly believed in himself, and his coaching record backed up that belief.

What we would come to understand about Wilf was that he had an inner passion for athletics, field or track, it didn't matter. His one goal was to make you better, even make you a world champion. He lived for athletics and every theory and practical session would be one of high intensity. He made you believe that you could be the next big thing in athletics.

However, I think I challenged his coaching ability when he insisted I could be the next great javelin thrower, only for me to throw distances that some primary schoolchildren could easily replicate. The same was true for my shot put and discus. When I asked him about the possibility of him coaching me in the hammer, he diplomatically announced that the PE college could not coach this due to health and safety regulations. He let me down softly!

His theory sessions were mesmerising as he quoted details of local, regional, national and world record distances and times. However, along with his passion and a clear strength of character, was a softer side.

Whenever any athletes were injured or thinking of retiring, Wilf would softly cajole them, and speak to them about their adverse predicaments. Then, when he sensed he had their full support to persevere through the injury or not retire, he would tell them to get a move on as the next up and coming world champion was about to take their place.

He was a master psychologist.

"Adversity in our life may seem like a problem, however, adversity can make us grow and learn, an opportunity that we may never have experienced. It all depends on how you look at it." Catherine Pulsifer. Canadian poet and writer whose work inspires people around the world.

SONOMA Waypoint Wisdom 22:

A one size fits all approach to adversity, where we must face it head-on and never give up, is only one approach.

SONOMA Waypoint Wisdom 23:

Our Frame of Reference will have a direct or indirect impact on our ability and response to tackling adversity. Do not judge yourself against others when fighting adversity.

SONOMA Waypoint Wisdom 24:

Your neuroplastic ability can be enhanced in later life to bring skills and talents to the fore. It's all about your Mindset. You can teach an old dog new tricks, but it's not as efficient as teaching a young dog new tricks!

SONOMA Waypoint Wisdom 25:

Sometimes to deal with adversity, we may have to lie low,

go under the radar, maybe sidle up alongside it and not be intimidated. We may decide to indulge in a few melancholy moments until we can face the challenge again.

SONOMA Waypoint Wisdom **26:**

It's the small steps that often lead to recovery. Never underestimate the power of small, incremental steps to success when giving support to others, but be patient and keep encouraging them.

SONOMA Waypoint Wisdom **27:**

Be proactive, i.e. do you have someone who will listen to you non-judgementally? Can you use this person to get your thoughts out and maybe get an alternative view, or just confirmation of your thinking?

SONOMA Waypoint Wisdom **28:**

Don't let over-expectations drive you. Be pragmatic and take your development in stages. Sometimes, expectations create and drive our internal narrative of how the world should respond to us. Be aware that your narrative might not be an appropriate one that will actually support you.

SONOMA Waypoint Wisdom **29:**

Don't be afraid to seek professional support, i.e. GP, therapists, other trained professionals. Often it is when we have a diagnosis that we know what we are dealing with, and it can be the first step into recovery.

SONOMA *Waypoint Wisdom* 30:

Writing thoughts and emotions down is a way to capture what's happening in your head and it can also be used to identify when you feel worse. It is a secure place to start your fight back.

SONOMA *Waypoint Wisdom* 31:

Are there things that you can do to make your situation better, i.e. socialising with people, outdoor activities, reducing or eliminating alcohol, stopping non-prescribed drugs, improving sleep hygiene, living with regular routines. Be patient. Things might take time but keep your belief and hope.

SONOMA *Waypoint Wisdom* 32:

When we support others we often feel a sense of well-being, a connectivity with our fellow humans and this can have a positive impact on our own mental health.

QR Code Express Conversations & Mind Exercises into...
Overcoming Challenges with Four Chairs

Measure your performance and add scores to the PSCP Matrix at the end of the book

Personal Sonoma Colour Profile –
3: Measurement of Strengths

I have adapted the '34 Themes of Strength Finder' (Buckingham & Clifton, 2001). By going through each of these strengths with a simple Yes or No, you will ascertain which areas are your strengths.

This is only a very simple adaptation, but it is a starting point for you to understand your strengths. It's not about having every one of these strengths, it is about you recognising *your* strengths:

For yourself, rate each word High, Medium or Low

Achiever – Catalyst – Adaptable
Analytical – Organised – Self-Belief
Manage Worries – Communicator – Competitive
Networker – Aware of Context – Diligent
Team Player – Disciplined – Empathetic
Fairness – Focused – Supportive
Harmony – Creative – Inclusiveness
Independent – Strategic – Knowledgeable
Learner – Maximise Opportunities – Positivity
Leadership – Responsible – Restorative
Confident – Detailed – Tactical

Scoring

Score each word either 3 high level, 2 medium level or 1 low level

Sonoma Gold = 67-99

You have enough strengths to be able to make an impact on your journey. The only challenge you may have is if others perceive you as being too strong and not showing any nice vulnerability like asking for advice, support or just canvassing others for opinions.

Sonoma Silver = 34-66

You have a good range of strengths and while there is always room for improvement, this mid-range balance may well suit your journey. Whilst supporting others try and ensure that you are not taken advantage of!

Sonoma Bronze = 1-33

Whilst you have some strengths, you probably need to work on possessing more. Clearly more strengths will make you more effective, but too many could mean you don't engage with others. Always involve others by sharing collective goals.

If you want a really accurate cross-reference measure, ask a peer to score you!

Summary of Spring

Spring is a time when the tide rushes onto the shore. It is powerful, rapid in nature and has a real surge of energy, intent and even a hint of menace. It is waiting to take you on a journey. The sooner you join the tide, the greater the distance you will travel. Any hesitation, or the taking of a wrong direction, may impede your progress.

Apply yourself and be open to new possibilities. Build your boat carefully, take instruction, pay attention to detail and it will not only keep you afloat, but it will guide you to reach the rewards of Summer and beyond.

Believe in yourself, be prepared to show some courage, maybe bravery in adversity, and trust in the journey even though you may be unsure of the destination. Spring is a time for aspiration, so let your reach exceed your grasp and roll that dice of life.

This time could specifically relate to being at school, college or university and taking exams, on an apprenticeship course, working as a trainee in a business environment, or even, unemployed and planning out your next move. Whatever you are doing or not doing, this is still a time where you can start to access your future life.

"Blossom by blossom, the Spring begins." Algernon Charles Swinburne (1837–1909) English poet, playwright, novelist, critic.

Summer

A time when everything comes into blossom and bloom.

A time when our hopes and dreams are made.

A time when we start to flourish and thrive.

A time when we sense our power, but don't yet know our capacity.

Summer, in terms of your journey to Sonoma, is a time to:

- Develop and polish your recently acquired knowledge and expertise.
- Learn the 'devil in the detail' and the power of focus.
- Be adaptable, consistent, reliable, and organised.
- 'Pivot' at a moment's notice.
- Understand and grow emotional confidence.
- Be more aware of empathetic and effective communication.
- Understand your impact on team performance.

Opportunities lay all around, seemingly endless options to explore, progress, and conquer. With the right support, guidance and patience, everything is within our grasp.

The Summer may be short, but the rewards could be exponential.

> "*And so with the sunshine and the great bursts of leaves growing on the trees, just as things grow in fast movies, I had that familiar conviction that life was beginning over again with the summer.*"
>
> F. Scott Fitzgerald, *The Great Gatsby*

Lesson 4:

The First Flower

Custodian of Details & Laser Focus

Hidden Story – Doris & Wishi, the Not So Dream Team

Doris was the CEO of the company. Being first was the name of the game for Doris. Wishi was her right-hand woman. Being right was the name of the game for Wishi.

Doris was a natural in so many ways. People gravitated to her friendly manner and were in awe of her determination, boldness, and decisiveness in getting things done. This allowed her to achieve so much, sometimes at the expense of others. She was a winner!

Wishi could be indecisive occasionally, and a plodder at times, but this was because she wanted to get her facts straight, and to fully understand the problem before she tackled it. People might tease her for being less confident, but her methodical and thorough style often helped her get there in the end and with everything in order.

One day, Doris assembled all the workers together. She had something important to reveal:

"We are going to tender for a really big contract from the government. If we get it, this will be the biggest contract our company has ever landed. It's really important we get this as it will safeguard our future. I will lead the bidding process."

Doris was going to land this deal and she picked Rees and Mogg to support her. They were loyal to her and would do as they were told and would never let her down.

Team Doris got to work bidding for this new contract. To ensure they got it, they followed the specifications, but added some extras, just in case another company pitched at the same level. After a week, Team Doris had put together a bid in record time. This was sent over immediately to the government, and they waited nervously for a response.

The very next day, a decision had been made. Doris addressed the staff:

"The government has accepted our bid. Now let's get right down to fulfilling it. I can see great times ahead for this company, just as long as everybody follows my lead," said Doris with a decisiveness in her voice, a steely glint in her eye and a swagger aimed at all those who had ever doubted her.

In due course, as the order was being fulfilled, some problems started to emerge. The added extras promised were not included and the government started to look more closely at the order itself. On inspection, the order was lacking a consistent quality, with some items in pristine condition, while others seemed to be second-rate.

Before long, the government was questioning other aspects of the order and found that the price had been increased and the delivery date extended beyond the agreed date. This was not what had been agreed. When they confronted Doris, she calmly said the deal had been signed and they had better put up or shut up!

The very next day the government gave an ultimatum to Doris – fix the order or lose the order. Doris refused to budge, and this made the rest of the workers nervous as losing this contract could see the whole company collapse. Noticing that all would be lost, Wishi swung into action. She got a company mandate to sack Doris and appointed her own team of Jeremy and Michael to revisit the bid, to put right all the false promises and to deliver on an honest contract.

She took her time as she wanted all the details to be correct and the government to be totally satisfied. This was where Wishi was superior to Doris – she had attention to detail, an honesty of business and a great supportive team behind her. The deal was renegotiated and delivered. Team Wishi reigned supreme for another year or so!

The moral of the story may be that no matter what personal skills or influence you may have, once you lose your attention to detail, all may be lost.

Global Story – Nolan Kapows Batman & Wachowskis' Matrix Twin X Factor

Attention to detail and laser-type focus are apparent in many walks of life, from within business, education, sports, and even relationships, to very specific cases, where life and reputation are in the balance, such as in medical operations, forensic evidence in a court room and pilots flying aeroplanes. However, a place where these qualities might have escaped your attention is in the movies.

Christopher Nolan is an acclaimed film director who has an obsessive eye for detail. In his movie, *The Dark Knight Rises*, Nolan had engineers and designers approach Batman's helicopter and Batmobile like actual military projects. He then made sure that the Batcave was a full-scale 360-degree replica set that could be submerged in a massive water tank.

He did not skimp on the smaller details either. Bane's jacket took two years to complete just so the designer could get the "dictatorial and revolutionary" balance just right. That's not even delving into the hundred-plus-piece Batsuit (and its many dozen replicas) that Nolan commissioned for the film.

The opening aerial sequence was filmed in a remote part of Scotland using actual airplanes and men parachuting and dangling from the planes. That Gotham stadium scene involved Nolan hiring hundreds of extras to fill the stadium. But all of that pales in comparison to the massive brawl at the movie's climax. Instead of pulling a Peter Jackson and relying on computer generated imaging or green screen, Nolan closed down Wall Street and hired thousands of extras to slug it out for a few days.

One other movie scene that comes close to that is in *The Matrix* which was directed by The Wachowskis. In the scene of *the Lady in the Red Dress* everybody in the background is a doppelgänger, i.e. they are all real-life twins. To get this effect, The Wachowskis spent a few days in Sydney scouting all the identical twins they could find in order to film that scene (Whatculture.com – Alexander Pan 2015).

Focus Under Pressure Neurosurgeons Help Violinist & Opera Singer

If you ever needed a more dramatic example of laser focus and attention to detail, look no further than the case of King's College neurosurgeon Keyoumars Ashkan and his patient Dagmar Turner.

Dagmar was a violinist, but had been diagnosed with a tumour in the right side of her brain. She was especially worried that the surgery to remove the tumour would affect not least, her ability to play with her dominant left hand. Dr Ashkan mapped out the different parts of Dagmar's brain as she played in the operating theatre. This took a painstaking two hours and then they proceeded to take away ninety per cent of the tumour. Dagmar made a complete recovery and still plays violin beautifully for the Isle Of Wight Symphony Orchestra.

In a similar story, neurosurgeon James Leggate had to operate on opera singer Russell Watson in 2006 when he had a brain tumour. Being entrusted to operate on a famous singer was real pressure, but it is something that neurosurgeons like James become accustomed to. However, any mistakes would almost certainly have curtailed Russell Watson's career, and maybe his life.

Laser focus and attention to detail saves lives.

My Story – PNE Trio Score a Hat Trick

For five years, between 1997 and 2002, I was community manager, then commercial manager, at Preston North End Football Club (PNEFC). In this time, I had three senior management figures who influenced my learning and development: Tony Scholes, CEO, Derek Shaw, chairman, and David Moyes, manager.

I learnt very quickly that each of them had not one, but two things in common: their attention to detail and their ability to focus on getting the right outcome. They displayed these traits in slightly different ways.

My immediate line manager was Tony Scholes, an accountant by training, but someone who had ascended quickly from club accountant to CEO in only a few years. He reported directly to the chairman and board of directors, and his role was to run the club, both on and off the pitch. Tony was perfect for this role.

On the playing side, when he was negotiating transfers, he was a stickler for reviewing the contracts, identifying all the 'hidden' riders, which left alone could cost the club in terms of an inflated purchase price, excessive percentage payouts to agents and even unfair stock devaluations when players left.

Equally, Tony was excellent at negotiating and renegotiating for club suppliers. I remember one such meeting, when we were negotiating with a brewery about them being the club's preferred supplier.

As commercial manager, my job was to bring the interested brewery to the negotiating table, discuss their delivery of products, timescales and unit costs. Tony's job was to do his homework first, by seeing what other breweries were prepared to pay and deliver, and then listen to what this brewery had in mind with a view to getting the best deal for PNE. We had a forty-five-minute meeting which was very relaxed. Tony let the brewery talk about its offer and listened to what they were *not* saying!

What this meant was that often, in negotiations around costs and value, the supplier can let slip their top line for securing the contract and which products cost them the least and have a high profit margin. Tony set up some scenarios around pint costs, different locations around the ground, short- and long-term contracts, etc. He was probing to see where they could lose some of their profit margins without it affecting them too greatly. These are the bits of a deal that have a high perceived value, but in reality, have relatively low cost attached.

When we came out of the meeting, not only did Tony know the top amount the brewery were prepared to pay for the contract, but also which parts of their service he could take advantage of without too much cost to the brewery. This is a classic win-win first famously described by Stephen Covey (2004).

In life, as we have seen from the previous lesson, it is best to focus on your strengths, and Tony did just that – his financial jousting was second to none at the club in those days. What made him so good was his research, his ability to pick out the key financial components of a deal and then get it over the line quickly, before the other party could change their mind! It is no surprise that Tony is now chief football officer for the Premier League.

Derek Shaw was the club chairman and a very successful self-made businessman. One of Derek's strengths was that he knew where every penny was going in his business. His primary strategy was to identify all his costs and then keep a close eye on them, even trying to reduce them at every opportunity.

He would then turn his attention to making money and securing profits. One of Derek's favourite sayings was 'don't be a busy fool' which meant 'don't spend forever doing things if those things do not deliver revenue'. He was constantly reminding me about my job title when I was not making enough money for the time I invested in a project.

Derek always had his finger on the financial pulse of the club. I think he knew more about the balance sheet than the club accountant. But beyond this, he was always focused on turning offers, deals and prospects into hard cash. Once, we were walking around the pitch on the eve of the new season and Derek was looking at all the new sponsorship boards I had in place. I was proud that each was filled, and some with new sponsors. He simply said:

> "Good job on filling all the sponsorship boards, Ross. But how many have been paid, and have we got all the money in our bank account yet?"

This was a salutary lesson: nothing is ever sold until *their* money is in *our* bank account.

David Moyes was the manager, or more commonly known as The Gaffer. As a club, we had known for some time that David had talent and our task would be to try to keep hold of him, as other larger clubs were circling to lure him away.

What made him a much sought-after target?

Quite simply, his almost obsessive attention to detail with player statistics, players' welfare (at a time when it wasn't overly analysed), playing strategies and tactics, transfer targets, equipment, playing surfaces, training facilities, etc.

David would always go the 'extra mile' to secure the right result, on or off the pitch.

I think at the time, he represented a new breed of manager who wanted to know everything about how to improve performance and left no stone unturned in his search for excellence.

This was evident when he decided to give me a dressing-down. My crime was to host the half-time entertainment of fun penalties on the pitch, more specifically, in the end that PNE would be attacking in the second half.

Looking back, I think David was successful because of his forensic intensity in those days, micro-managing every detail of the playing side. These days he seems to have changed some aspects of his management style, maybe as a result of having more staff and resources at his disposal.

Perhaps, like Sir Alex Ferguson, he had to establish himself and his ways first within an organisation, then and only then, could he adopt a more relaxed macro-management, hands off-style in some areas.

This journey to management excellence makes him still a much sought-after manager.

Deep Dive – Custodian of Details & Laser Focus – Dr Donald Lays Down the Rules

A custodian of details and laser focus are terms which most people understand, but it is difficult to provide exact evidence of how this works in real life. However, here are two examples that shed some light on the applied process.

Barack Obama appointed Dr Donald M Berwick to serve as the administrator of the centres for Medicare and Medicaid Services in 2010. Prior to this he had a successful career as a healthcare professional and by 1983 he was appointed Vice President of Quality-of-Care Measurement at Harvard Community Health Plan.

In that role he studied and experienced in great depth, the impact of healthcare management on people's lives. He used scientific methods, evidence-based research and comparative effectiveness research to improve the trade-off between quality, safety and costs. With his team, he had analysed patient care with the kinds of analytical tools that were akin to those used to assess the quality of cars coming off a production line!

His attention to detail was simply phenomenal. In one of his most famous interventions, he discovered the 'defect' rate in healthcare was as high as one in ten, meaning, for example, that ten per cent of patients were experiencing poor care. This was a shockingly high defect rate – many other industries had managed to achieve performance at levels of one error in one thousand cases (and often far better).

Berwick knew that the high medical defect rate meant that tens of thousands of patients were dying every year, unnecessarily. His conclusion was that hospitals could benefit from the same kind of rigorous process improvements that had worked in other industries. Could a transplant operation be 'produced' as consistently and flawlessly as a Toyota Camry? Berwick's ideas were so well supported by research that they were essentially indisputable, yet little was happening.

On December 14, 2004, he gave a speech to a room full of hospital administrators at a large industry convention:

"Here is what I think we should do. I think we should save one hundred thousand lives. And I think we should do that by June 14, 2006 – eighteen months from today. Some is not a number; soon is not a time. Here's the number: one hundred thousand. Here's the time: June 14, 2006 – 9am."

He proposed six very specific, medically detailed interventions to save lives such as elevating the heads of patients on ventilators, monitoring warning signs and sharing good practice. He shared these interventions with hospitals who signed up to the scheme. Once enrolled, his team showed the hospitals how to embrace the new interventions.

Team members provided research, step-by-step instruction guides, and training. They arranged conference calls for hospital leaders to share their victories and struggles with one another. They encouraged hospitals with early successes to become 'mentors' to hospitals just joining the campaign.

By staying laser-focused on these six interventions, and adopting the wraparound procedures, Berwick made sure the healthcare professionals administering these changes were not exhausted and had the clarity of understanding required. Slowly but surely, lives were beginning to be saved on a large scale. Eighteen months later, at the exact moment he had promised to return, Berwick took the stage again to announce the results:

"Hospitals enrolled in the One Hundred Thousand Lives Campaign have collectively prevented an estimated 122,300 avoidable deaths and, as importantly, have begun to institutionalise new standards of care that will continue to save lives and improve health outcomes into the future." (Adapted from Wikipedia internet sources & Chip & Dan Heath, 2010).

Custodian of Details & Laser Focus – Remember Jay Cross?

If you are looking for somebody who needed to demonstrate attention to detail and laser focus under pressure, then surely that person would be somebody who had to remember facts for a living – a 'memory champion'. I came across this person when I was delivering Memory Training for School exams. I had completed my prior learning and built up my resources, but then a thought occurred to me. If I want to talk about having a great memory, then surely, I should talk to an actual memory champion and see what was really involved.

I researched several people, and eventually secured an online meeting with former world memory champion Jay Cross. What he told me in ten minutes has stayed with me my entire life. He said that anyone could be a world memory champion. It was just a matter of knowing which systems worked for you, having enough time to practise and having enough motivation to persist.

We talked about specific ways to memorise like acronyms, mnemonics, mind maps, visual and word association, memory paths that replicate your own world, and the Loci Method. He even told me the story of Simonides of Ceos, an ancient Greek, who was having a party in his house when a great fire broke out, killing many guests. When he was asked to list who was there, he could not remember anyone. But then he went back in his mind, to revisit each of the rooms and visualised each of his guests (this is the Loci Method).

Jay then went on to tell me another key piece of information:

"If you want to be a world memory champion, or a champion in life, you need to be a custodian of knowledge. you must seek it everywhere: in books, on websites, in connections with people, reading blogs and delivering vlogs, writing papers. You will know when you have achieved your goal of being a champion when people start coming to you for advice and help!"

As an amusing aside, when I first logged on to my virtual interview with Jay, I saw him frantically looking for something on his desk. He then muttered to himself:

"Now where did I put that pack of playing cards?"

But how do we develop a razor-sharp memory?

A key component of memorising something is the process of remembering, or recall. You must practise recalling information quickly after you have first learnt it. An analogy of this could be walking across a field and a path is formed, i.e. learning. If you walk across the same path the following day, you can make the path more visible.

Each day you are creating a clearer path to walk along, until eventually the path is established and requires no effort to find it. If, though, you do not walk down it again for a few days, maybe a week, the path may have started to become overgrown, and it may be difficult to find. The same happens with our memory.

Jay Cross talked about specific time periods when memory is lost. After one hour of learning, you can lose up to twenty per cent of that knowledge. After a day it rises to forty per cent, a week sixty per cent and by the end of a month it reaches eighty per cent!

To stop this happening, it is important to recall something immediately and then practise recalling it for a few weeks until it sticks. Then all you have to do is recall it now and again to check you have still remembered it.

Explicit semantic knowledge (stored facts and general knowledge of the world) is thought to reside in the frontal cortex as long-term memories. But initial memories, at the start of learning, are made and stored in the hippocampus before eventual deposit in the frontal cortex. This makes the work of the hippocampus crucial when we are first learning something.

The hippocampus can also affect learning when it is un-motivated, and this lack of motivation makes learning and recalling more difficult. Equally, if we are nervous, the amygdala, which is situated next to the hippocampus in the limbic system area of the brain, can interrupt learning by hijacking this pathway and flooding the frontal cortex, making memory almost impossible... remember being so nervous you could hardly speak, perhaps meeting a superstar, or a person who you like?

Renowned memory expert Tony Buzan (2009) often talked about mental literacy and how you can take advantage of mnemonics and mind mapping. He explained the view that your brain is a *Sleeping Giant* – it just needs to be woken up and then life really does open up. Remember, memory can be taught and improved.

Challenge

Yes, memory can be improved by using various techniques. But no matter which techniques you use, if you have little motivation and invest only small amounts of time, even the most gifted amongst us will struggle to recall information, especially over longer periods of time. It's all about stimulating the hippocampus.

Famous Example of Attention to Detail – Fred Eyre Boosts his Business With Paper Clips

Every match day at PNEFC, I would host the hospitality areas as well as the pitch-side communications. One Saturday it was my pleasure to welcome former player and manager Fred Eyre who had played for twenty clubs up until the age of thirty-eight.

Fred was, and still is, a marvellous raconteur, but what many did not know was that he presided over a very successful office supplies business. This was revealed to the three hundred-plus crowd when somebody asked him how he made it:

"In the early days, I was scrambling around for

orders, trying to get the office supplies business off the ground. I had some premises in an old women's prison costing me fifteen shillings a week (seventy-five pence) and my secretary was my mother who received the business orders direct to her home phone.

I was always focused on the details of the business, from knowing about all the possible items that could be sold, to being reliable on delivery. I traded on my stock phrase, 'no matter how small, we will deliver on the same day'.

Then one day I received an order from Mr Jackson for a box of paper clips. Not only was it a tiny order which would net me three shillings (one and a half pence), but it had to be delivered to King Street which was an unsavoury area of Manchester where you could be robbed in broad daylight for a bit of spare change, the exact same change for which I was working.

Nevertheless, and true to my word, I dropped off the paper clips. Not only did I receive my payment, but Mr Jackson also placed another order for three swivel chairs, three desks, and a filing cabinet, with a total value of one hundred and twenty pounds!

In my eagerness to deliver, I purchased the items and drove to the King Street building. Then it hit me... how do I, on my own, carry all this equipment up to the offices? As I sat on the tail-lift of the vehicle, worrying, a friendly face appeared. It was none other than legendary footballer and friend, Denis Law.

> *Within a few minutes we had delivered the items and I had got paid. On the way out I overheard Mr Jackson saying 'That Fred Eyre is going places. He's even got Denis Law working for him!'.*"

The story above wasn't the original story I had written. After asking Fred to give me permission to use it, he telephoned me to say, very nicely, that I had mixed up two stories. We started talking about the best story to use when he interrupted me and said he was coming over to Preston to sort everything out.

If ever a story demonstrated a definitive example of attention to detail, Fred Eyre was the epitome of that principle, especially as he was coming all the way from Manchester to make sure I had the correct details.

Elton John is Still Standing for Details

Attention to detail and laser focus are also necessary in other aspects of life. At Glastonbury 2023, these qualities were evident on the set of Elton John. *The Independent* (June 26, 2023) described it as 'an incredible Glastonbury headline show' and it featured Elton in a resplendent gold suit and red-tinted glasses, playing an incredibly diverse array of old and new songs, interjected with choreographed guest appearances under an amazing array of stage lights and backdrop fireworks.

Other singers such as Pink with her stunning acrobatic routines and Beyoncé with her dance productions, also fall into this category of attention to detail and laser focus.

"When the sun is shining, I can do anything; no mountain is too high, no trouble is too difficult to overcome." Wilma Rudolph (1940–1994) African American sprinter who overcame childhood polio to become a world record-holding Olympic athlete.

SONOMA *Waypoint Wisdom* 33:

Possessing a laser focus and attention to detail can set you apart from other professionals and a positive reputation can be built upon this. It is often the pursuit and use of detail that separates professionals.

SONOMA *Waypoint Wisdom* 34:

Sometimes attention to detail is focusing on what someone does not say or omits from a conversation or a report. Being able to pinpoint missing pieces of information or omissions may allow you to negotiate with people or interrogate data more effectively.

SONOMA *Waypoint Wisdom* 35:

Attention to detail can seem unimportant, but never underestimate the impact little details can have on the big picture.

SONOMA *Waypoint Wisdom* 36:

Being the custodian of knowledge from a variety of sources may well give you the professional edge which can ultimately lead you to become seen as the industry expert.

SONOMA Waypoint Wisdom 37:

The longer you leave it to recall information, the harder that process becomes. Recall information regularly, especially when you first learn it.

SONOMA Waypoint Wisdom 38:

The secret to possessing a good memory is to be motivated and enjoy learning. Once you start to do this, nerves will disappear and there is less chance of an amygdala hijack.

SONOMA Waypoint Wisdom 39:

Your memory capacity and power is largely unlimited. Be prepared to put some memory work in, but be creative with your memory practices as this will keep you interested and motivated.

QR Code Express Conversations & Mind Exercises into...
Remember It Like Beckham

Measure your performance and add scores to the PSCP Matrix at the end of the book

Personal Sonoma Colour Profile –
4: Measurement of Memory

So, let's set a challenge that uses visual association, stories and acronyms as a memory aid. This technique could help you in all sorts of ways to remember key information, especially when put under the spotlight of performance.

Here is a list of the Top Ten Dad Jokes (I will apologise now for the lack of funniness). I will then give you some systems that you can adapt to make the recalling of information easier.

For now, just try and remember each joke.

1. The graveyard must be overcrowded – people must be dying to get in.
2. I am reading a book about anti-gravity – it is impossible to put down.
3. What do you call a magician who has lost their magic? – Ian.
4. I used to hate facial hair – but then it grew on me.
5. My wife said, are you ever going to stop singing 'Wonderwall'? – I said, 'Maybe'.
6. I like to go backwards – but only when I put the car in reverse.
7. I only know twenty-five letters of the alphabet – I don't know Y.
8. Dad, can you put my shoes on? – No, I don't think they fit me.

9. How do I look? – With your eyes.

10. I am on a Yo-Yo Diet – my weight goes up and down.

Scoring

Each remembered joke scores 1 point.

Now try a little practice to see how many you can remember – we are stimulating the hippocampus, so we must be motivated, and relax as we do not want the amygdala hijacking you. This might be your way of remembering.

Here are some other ways that can be used.

Visual Cue & Theme

Imagine you are walking down the road and there are a number of shops on the high street. These will give you a trigger memory boost to remember the joke.

1. **U**ndertakers
2. **B**ook Shop
3. **M**agic Shop
4. **H**airdressers
5. **R**ecord Shop
6. **C**ar Mechanics
7. **A**lphabet Baby Shop
8. **S**hoe Shop
9. **O**pticians
10. **T**oy Shop

Now try and make a story up of you walking down the high street, the sillier and weirder you make it, the easier it is to remember.

Acronym Support
In order, the first letter of each shop is **UBMHRCASOT**. But this may be hard to remember. So, I have rearranged the letters to something more memorable, i.e. easier to remember.

UMB – CHARSOT
I now just recall each shop to each letter and hopefully the joke is waiting for me in the shop! But again, you must practise it by trying to remember UMB first, then adding C, and so on.

If it is any consolation, this is a hard task, mainly because the human mind usually can only remember up to seven items. So let us see if you are superhuman?

Scoring

Sonoma Gold = 8-10
You have an excellent memory. If you are motivated and completed a few practices this will have undoubtedly created your high score. To maintain this knowledge, you must keep testing yourself every now and again.

Sonoma Silver = 5-7
You have a good memory. Did you practise enough, were you motivated to remember, were you distracted? If you want to improve, think about what you need to do differently next time.

Sonoma Bronze = 1-4
Below average memory but the good news is that you can certainly improve. Maybe work with a friend to test you

step by step, or joke by joke. If you want to be better, it is just down to finding a practice method that works for you and your brain.

Lesson 5:

A Race to Bloom

Consistency, Immediate Adaptability,
Environment & Smart Resilience

Hidden Story – Has the Penny Dropped for the Daughters?

A father is teaching his two young daughters the ways of the world. He wants to prepare them for life when he is gone, but also to teach them some key skills, which if mastered, will keep repaying both daughters as they grow older. He can tell them what to do or not to do, but rather, prefers to teach them with choices and consequences. One day, he asks the same question to both of them:

"Which would you rather have, three million dollars right now, or receive a cent that doubles every day for thirty-one days?"

The first daughter immediately says she would like the three million dollars. The second daughter opts for a cent doubling every day for thirty-one days.

After Day 5 the second daughter has only sixteen cents. Even on Day Ten it's only 5.12 dollars. After twenty days, the second daughter still only has 5,243 dollars compared to three million dollars and there are only eleven days left.

On Day 29, the total is now 2.7 million dollars, which is still less than three million dollars. However, like many things in life, the last part of the journey can reveal the greatest rewards. On Day 31, the penny has grown to 10,737,418.24 dollars (Darren Hardy, 2010).

The moral I take from this story is that in life we have to be consistent in our good behaviours if we want success that endures. These small steps of progress help to build momentum. Equally, we must have belief that our chosen path is the right one.

Global Story – Simpson Gets in a Tangle... Doh!

In 1985, English mountaineers Joe Simpson and Simon Yates reached the summit of Siula Grande in the Peruvian Andes via the previously unclimbed West Face. On their descent, Yates accidentally stepped onto an overhanging ledge of snow and fell down the mountain.

His safety rope saved him from falling 4,500 feet to his certain death. Simpson hauled him up to relative safety on a ridge still high on the mountainside. Both climbers were tiring, and with the weather turning nasty, and the light starting to fade, they decided to spend the night on the ridge, which meant using up the last of their food rations. No matter what happened now, they had to get off the mountain the following day.

Continuing their descent the following morning, Simpson fell from an ice cliff and landed awkwardly, breaking his right leg and crushing his tibia and his knee joint. With bad weather closing in and daylight fading, they needed to descend quickly to the glacier, about three thousand feet below.

Yates proceeded to lower Simpson off the North Ridge using their two one-hundred-and-fifty-foot ropes tied together to make one three-hundred-foot rope, controlling the speed at which he lowered Simpson using a belay plate. This was an unorthodox method which involved lowering for one hundred and fifty feet before they had to rethread the rope to allow Simpson to travel another one hundred and fifty feet down the mountainside. This also meant that Yates had to move down the mountain each time.

This improvised course of action carried on for almost three thousand feet and they were almost safe until Simpson went off the end of another cliff and dangled in mid-air. He was stuck and Yates was also stuck as he could not rescue him. For over an hour and a half they were fixed in this state until Yates could not hold his position. He had no choice but to cut the rope and hope Simpson didn't have far to fall. Simpson plummeted down the cliff and into a deep crevasse.

Though exhausted and suffering from hypothermia, he was still alive. He dug himself into a snow hole. From there, Simpson spent three days without food and with almost no water, hopping and finally crawling five miles back to their base camp. Blisteringly hot during the day, and freezing at night, he kept adapting to the climate and terrain.

Exhausted and delirious, he reached base camp only a few hours before Yates and Richard Hawking (the third member of the group, a non-climber) intended to leave the base camp and return to civilisation.

Simpson's story is regarded by mountaineers as amongst the most remarkable instances of survival against the odds. Both climbers had to adapt immediately to ever-changing situations to save their lives (Joe Simpson, 1998).

> *Have you ever been in a dangerous situation that needed quick adaptability to resolve imminent danger?*

The Young Shuffle

Another lesser-known story that incorporates aspects of consistency, immediate adaptability, environment and smart resilience is the curious case of Australian potato and sheep farmer, and amateur runner, Albert Ernest Clifford Young.

In 1983, aged sixty-one, Cliff Young entered the inaugural Westfield Sydney to Melbourne Ultramarathon, a distance of five hundred and forty-four miles. Strangely, Young arrived to compete in overalls and work boots, and without his dentures as he complained that they rattled when he ran! He even told reporters before the race, that for the previous two or three nights he had been rounding up sheep in his gumboots.

What also marked out Cliff Young as different was that he ran at a slow pace, shuffling along, and some suggested that this was some sort of publicity stunt. After the first day, he trailed the pack by a large margin. However, while the other competitors stopped to sleep for six hours, Cliff Young kept on running through the night.

In the morning he was in the lead and after continuous running at a steady pace of around four miles per hour, he finished in a time of five days, fifteen hours and four minutes. This placed him first, a staggering ten hours ahead of the next competitor. This was a course record-beating the previous time by almost two days.

When asked about his mental strategy during his post-event press conference, he said he simply imagined he was running after sheep trying to outrun a storm. When he received the prize money of ten thousand dollars he said he wasn't aware that there was prize money. He felt bad, so he shared it between the other five runners, taking none for himself.

The 'Young Shuffle' has since been copied by other ultramarathon runners as it expended less energy, with at least three winners adopting it for the Westfield Sydney to Melbourne race. Albert Ernest Clifford Young ran races up to his late seventies, achieving a world age record in 2000 aged seventy-eight in a six-day race in Victoria. He died on November 2nd, 2003, aged eighty-one. There is a memorial to him in the shape of a gumboot (Wikipedia, Cliff Young).

Can you think of a better example of somebody who adapted uniquely to his environment, was consistent and used smart resilience?

Matthew Jordan Smiles Through the Rain

A simpler example of immediate adaptability can be found with golfer Matthew Jordan. He was playing in the 151st

Open in 2023 at his home club of Hoylake, Merseyside, and it was the first club he joined, aged seven. Now, twenty years later, he was on the biggest golfing stage of his life.

Heavy persistent rain meant conditions were pretty miserable. But Matthew had a big smile on his face, and almost looked like he was enjoying the horrible conditions. He switched his emotions. Nothing, not least the appalling weather, was going to spoil his opportunity of playing and performing in front of his home crowd. It is no coincidence that this positive adaptable attitude also secured him a top ten finish amongst the world's finest golf stars. His attitude reminded me of another literary gem which we could all do to remember:

"*Wherever you go, no matter what the weather is, always bring your own sunshine.* Anthony J D'Angelo (author and public speaker).

My Story – Saudi Arabian Military Aircraft Bases – Thunderbirds Are Go!

In 1987 I started working for the United States Sports Academy (USSA) in Saudi Arabia on several Royal Saudi Air Force (RSAF) military bases. My job title was sports generalist coach which meant I had to teach a variety of sports and leisure-type activities to military personnel and their children, at a variety of bases, and times. Sometimes this would be all through the night during Ramadan, or at sunrise, just for one hour of training before it became too hot.

To do this effectively, I had to be inducted, not only

into understanding my coaching role, and how the multimillion-dollar facilities operated, but to the wider personnel responsibilities that included Arabic culture and customs. This was critical for two reasons.

Firstly, USSA had invested heavily in a global recruitment programme and potential candidates had gone through a series of tests before being recruited. Once in the designated coaching role, you were upskilled on a mastery programme and shown how to operate as a team overseas. In a few short weeks, we had received the required training and were regarded by USSA as prized assets of high worth who would give long-standing service.

Secondly, and perhaps more importantly, you were inducted onto the Arabia programme. This was a series of workshops that explained Arabic custom, culture and basic communication language. We were taught how to behave on base, and off base, within each town or city.

Our staff retention rates were always above ninety per cent and contracts were often rolled over year after year, keeping staff in place and ensuring a consistent high-quality service to the RSAF. This integrated organisational approach to employment was comprehensive. It taught me that no matter how good you thought you were, you had to know fully the system or environment within which you were working.

Those environmental skills have stayed with me to this day, in particular, being dialled into your specific location. Knowing the rules and consequences, understanding the policies and procedures to the letter, as your life, and others, could depend upon it.

Back in the UK, what did that experience teach me that I could apply in any working environment I encountered? It taught me that you had to fully understand your environment, so you could be effective, not fall foul of the system, and ultimately, you could take advantage of it. What do I mean by that? If it was education, this meant being diligent in learning school policies and procedures. It meant being aware of individual pupil profiles. It meant knowing the school reward and sanctions approach. Once you were dialled into the specific environment, you could then play by the rules and keep ahead of the game.

Saudi Arabia also taught me that different customs and cultures do exist and need to be understood and respected. However, on one occasion, a new member of the support staff who had just arrived on base decided to be a practical joker. At the last prayer at around 9pm, many hundreds of Muslims went to pray at the local mosque. All those who entered this mosque had to remove their shoes and wash their feet. The new recruit thought it would be a good idea to sneak down and rearrange the hundreds of pairs of shoes, so that when everyone was leaving they would struggle to find their own.

What seemed like a silly joke soon turned serious as many people upon leaving the mosque started to argue and tempers flared. Very quickly the local police arrived, and the finger of blame pointed to our adjacent villa. Soon afterwards, the offending recruit was led away, imprisoned overnight and was on a plane back to the USA the following day. He was lucky. That same thinking of respecting customs and cultures applies in today's schools, where you can be presented with multi-faiths, different sexualities, different statemented emotional needs, and complicated family histories.

Over the years, I have worked in over 1,500 schools, colleges and universities. Knowing each of those environments, often at short notice if I was supply-teaching, was crucial to my success. When most supply teachers were tucking into tea and toast in the staffroom before lessons began, I was studying school policy, rules, sanctions and rewards and learning which pupils had a reputation for disruption!

Have you ever prepared yourself for an upcoming challenge, where without such preparation, the outcome night have been different?

Deep Dive – Smart Resilience – Dr Rick Is Thriving

Resilience is something professionals of most ages understand as being durable, bounce-back ability and just keeping on going. As Winston Churchill said:

"When you're going through hell, just keep going."

I have been brought up on this mantra and I have indeed developed resilience through tough times. But I have experienced a series of panic attacks as a result of being too resilient for too long. I have also seen what being resilient has done to other people who have tried to fight the 'good fight' but then developed severe mental health challenges as a result of this approach.

Often terms like resilience have a historical and cultural root, in as much as we are expected to do what our predecessors did, what our society expects, what our peers demand. We should 'just get on with it' or 'what doesn't kill you makes you stronger', or worse still, 'just man up'. There is a danger that this can be damaging for both the individual and a collective organisation.

A recognised and established world leader on resilience is Dr Rick Hansen. He is a senior fellow at the University of California, Berkeley's Greater Good Science Centre, has published several books, is a *Times* best-selling author and his podcasts have been downloaded over nine million times. Hansen describes resilience as being multifaceted and it's not just all about what most textbooks quote resilience as, i.e. 'bounce-back ability', 'keep going' and 'never give up'.

He has a wider description that includes the ability to feel compassion for self, mindfulness, learning, confidence, gratitude, motivation, aspiration, and courage. Or more succinctly, Hansen informs us that it is not all boom and bust, or just relentlessly driving forward. Moreover, he describes it as:

> "*Resilience is not about surviving every day; it's about thriving every day. To do this, we must look after our own mental health. We must be compassionate with ourselves, mindful of our triggers, stresses, joyous moments, build our resources and support systems. Crucially, we need to know our limits.*" (Rick Hansen, 2018).

Interestingly, when I attended one of his online webinars, one thing struck me immediately and stayed with me for the duration of the online seminar. He was incredibly relaxed. I guess at aged seventy plus, he knew how to handle life and his body's responses to life.

Individually, we are all slightly different in terms of genetics, experienced environment, experience of trauma (especially when we are younger), sex, sexuality, age, religious bias, cultural expectations, education, work responsibilities, family responsibilities, etc. (Frame of Reference.) Again, as with adversity, this is why we cannot have a 'one size fits all' approach to resilience.

Equally, our moods and situations can change daily and so what we could push through and do today, might be different given the same challenge tomorrow. We need to be more fluid in our approach to resilience, we need to understand it is multifaceted, and we must not judge the ability of others to produce resilience, as we do not know everything about them and their own Frame of Reference. This is what I term 'smart resilience'.

Smart resilience means to keep trying and pushing, being adaptable, but recognising when you or others might need support, might need a break, might need another direction and focus. It's about checking in with yourself constantly, weighing up how you feel, maybe stepping back and refuelling or stepping towards a challenge boldly. We all need to keep taking our internal temperature, or as Rick Hansen explained online, pinching a quote from Stephen Covey... "*Give yourself psychological oxygen.*"

Try not to hang onto old and sometimes dangerous

aphorisms around resilience – everybody's situation, resources and Frame of Reference history may be different.

Challenge

Maybe we need to know our limits first or where the boundaries are, so we know where not to go next time, or go there with more experience, more support and more resources.

Is the Canary Still Singing?

Collective expectations of resilient behaviour can often be found in many larger organisations. They see resilience as a 'must have' company quality. The management set out to upskill everybody in resilient behaviours. There is an expectation that everyone will display resilience in every aspect of their work which in turn will make the company grow and be more profitable.

Given what we now know about Frame of Reference, could this be disastrous organisationally? Mariam Alexander writing for *The Guardian* (March 2021) talked about the qualities of the NHS, and how it had to be robust and resilient to cope with the extra demands of the pandemic.

What she noticed was that certain cohorts of the organisation were very adept at changing or adapting to the new pandemic demands and could switch into more resilient behaviours to work longer hours, take shorter breaks and take on more responsibilities.

However, there were many others who struggled with this change, who had adverse responses to consistently witnessing multiple deaths and severe illness at close quarters. Not only were they struggling to adapt and cope, but they were made to feel, consciously or subconsciously, inferior to those who could adapt and manage. She likened this to the 'canary in the cage syndrome'.

This dated back to mining times when miners used to take a canary down the mines. The canary was renowned for its constant singing and talking. However, if it stopped talking and singing there was a good chance that methane, a naturally occurring gas often detected underground, had poisoned it.

Returning to those good employees, who could not fully adapt to the pandemic, they were like the canary that was dying, but nobody noticed these groups. So, whether it's individually or collectively, be careful that we do not become weak because we have tried to display too much resilience, for too long, with too much intensity. We are all made differently and exist with varying stresses and responsibilities. Do not be too quick to judge, or better still, don't judge at all.

Have you ever reflected and recognised that you have been over-resilient at times?

Deep Dive – Immediate Adaptability – Pivot like Joe Wicks & HR Steve

Adaptability is having the knack to change to a new situation or new demand, or try a different approach to an existing scenario. Sometimes we need to do this immediately, as was the case during the pandemic. Many people and organisations had to adapt, and do it quickly. Essential products such as hand sanitisers, masks and general PPE were either made or imported at record speed. People had to adjust to new working conditions, demands and controls.

The work from home (WFH) scenario was a completely new way of working for many. Face-to-face activities were transferred online from board meetings of multinational companies down to how we exercised, including TV personality, Joe Wicks. Overnight we became a nation of *Celebrity Squares*, all in 'boxes' on screens.

The ones who thrived in this new environment were those who were able to *pivot* quickly to the changes. Some put services online for the first time or invested in better broadband speed. Others created more or improved existing online resources, and many became familiar with the virtual facilities provided by software programmes like Zoom and Teams. *Pivot* people ruled. Joe Wicks ruled.

He pivoted again when he branched out into heath foods and cookery.

I recently witnessed an example of immediate adaptability within the corporate world. I was hosting a session on mental health development with ten high-flyers in London for NTT Global.

I was facilitating conversations around the effectiveness of the employee assistance programme (EAP) when a person said that the portal to the system threw up too many barriers and actually prevented people accessing crucial support. Specifically, it was taking too long to speak to an expert.

The Head of Human Resources, Steve Warner, stood up and left the room. Within less than a minute he had returned:

"No more delays in the portal – problem fixed!"

A perfect corporate example of immediately adaptability.

Famous Example of Immediate Adaptation – Mr Carrott Quietly Wins Over the Audience, but Loses

In 2001, PNEFC were playing Birmingham City in the second leg of the Division One play-off semi-finals. The winner would go to Wembley to contest the play-off final and be in with a chance of being promoted to the Premier League.

For such an auspicious occasion, I booked Jasper Carrott, a well-known comedian who was also a superfan of Birmingham City. I introduced him to the three hundred guests in The Great Room, who were mainly PNE supporters, and the reception, as you could imagine, was one of 'friendly' banter. Jasper was starting on the back foot, but you would not have noticed it. Almost immediately, though, the microphone started to fail. Now he had a baying crowd and no voice to win them round.

What did he do?

He adapted by asking all the waiting staff to stop what they were doing for ten minutes, as their background noise was affecting the ability of the audience to hear him. He then told me to get a replacement microphone whilst he talked a little more loudly and moved around the room so most people could hear him at some point. He told quick-fire jokes to each section of the room. Pure genius.

After a few minutes, the replacement microphone was in place, and he addressed the room in a cheeky manner:

"I use that trick every time I go to entertain visiting fans. The quietness of the room makes the barrackers go quiet. If they give me banter, nobody can hear the jokes."

He had adapted immediately and beautifully to the environment, both in terms of being heard and getting people on his side. It was a pity the result did not go his way as PNEFC won.

In his haste to leave, he forgot his twenty bottles of champagne, which he had put on ice to toast victory. The good news was that they were enjoyed by PNEFC players and staff.

"Adaptability is being able to adjust to any situation at any given time." John Wooden (1910–2010). American basketball coach and player. He won ten National Collegiate Athletic Association Championships in a twelve-year period as head coach for the UCLA Bruins, including seven in a row.

SONOMA Waypoint Wisdom 40:

In life you should not only choose wisely, but you should persist over time. This consistency of behaviour may often feel quite mundane, even boring. But good decisions and actions multiplied over time can yield staggering results.

SONOMA Waypoint Wisdom 41:

As a professional, you may be called upon to be adaptable at some point in your career. Have the belief and conviction to introduce new ideas and establish new trends. This could lead to a new level of success. You will know when this adaptive attitude is really successful when others copy you.

SONOMA Waypoint Wisdom 42:

If you do not know the rules, and do not fully understand how to maximise this knowledge, then you are ultimately destined to fail.

SONOMA Waypoint Wisdom 43:

The secret to resilience is to try and challenge your power and capacity, but ensure you have good support systems with people around you who have realistic expectations. You will need to recognise when you are struggling, and maybe change your approach. This is being adaptable. Don't see it as a weakness or flaw if you cannot perform as expected.

SONOMA Waypoint Wisdom 44:

The ability to pivot will set you apart from others. Sometimes this pivot needs to be quick, responsive and large-scaled.

QR Code Express Conversations & Mind Exercises into...
Smart Resilience

Measure your performance and add scores to the PSCP Matrix at the end of the book

Personal Sonoma Colour Profile –
5: Measurement of Smart Resilience

Classic tests of resilience are often based solely on the survive logic. Whilst these tests may be valid and accurate, I feel many do not address the aspects of thrive resilience which Dr Rick Hansen talked about. Sometimes being too resilient for too long can make us un-resilient, brittle and burnt out.

Below is my Smart Resilience Test which takes into account mental health that incorporates an ability to thrive and demonstrate sustainable resilience.

Smart Resilience
Answer Always, Sometimes or Never
1. I love to take on a challenge and give it my best shot.
2. I don't recognise when I am pushing too much, for too long, too often.
3. To help me succeed, I rarely access support as that makes me less independent.
4. I am aware when I tire and need a break or need to get help.
5. I can give up easily on certain projects.
6. I am aware when my mental health starts to be impacted.
7. I can push myself when I feel resilient, but know when to be adaptable when I am not feeling resilient.
8. I can be indecisive.

Scoring
Questions 1, 4, 6, 7
Always = 2, Sometimes = 1, or Never = 0

Questions 2, 3, 5, 8
Always = 0 , Sometimes = 1, or Never = 2

Sonoma Gold = 7-8
You have smart resilience. You can push yourself through challenges, but you know when it's okay to back off and maybe recharge and review. You have a good balance between pushing and stepping back.

Sonoma Silver = 3-6
You possess a good level of smart resilience. It could be that you are very aware of pushing yourself too much, or it could be a case of just taking on more challenges with support.

Sonoma Bronze = 0-2
Your smart resilience can be improved. Maybe look at the areas where you scored lower than the rest to assess your specific areas for improvement. Maybe try to take on challenges, but remember, don't push yourself too much too soon, at the expense of your mental health.

Lesson 6:

The Blossoming Vista

Emotional Intelligence, Empathetic Active Listening & Direct Communication

Hidden Story – Freddie Fixes it For a Punch

Freddy Fixer did not have a bad bone in his body. All he wanted to do was help people. He thought he was very good at this, and believed he could fix anything. One day, his friend Jenny came round to see him. She was upset and weeping uncontrollably.

"What's the matter, Jenny?" said Freddy Fixer, eager to know what the problem was so he could fix it.

"My ninety-two-year-old grandmother has just died!"

"Oh well, she had a good innings!" said Freddy, trying to comfort her.

Jenny started to cry more loudly. Freddy then tried another response.

"Well, at least you have another grandmother."

Jenny continued to cry.

Freddy Fixer had made things worse, *but not to worry*, he thought, *at least I tried.*

Across the road, Mickey had his head in his hands, sat on the kerbside, and a dog collar by his side.

"Cheer up, Mickey, it might not happen," said Freddy, trying to be funny.

"My dog just got run over and died," said Mickey.

"We'll get you another, what sort do you want?" said Freddy.

Mickey threw the dog collar at Freddy and stomped off.

Freddy Fixer was not having a good day, but that would not stop him trying to fix things. Waking down the road was Harriet. Freddy sidled up beside her.

"Where you off to, Harriet?" said Freddy.

"I'm down, and depressed," replied Harriet.

"I'm depressed too!" replied Freddy.

Freddy then proceeded to tell, or rather, talk at Harriet, telling her about all his problems, hijacking her thoughts and emotions and putting the attention on himself. When he had finished, Freddy added,

"Well, at least there are other people worse off than you, Harriet. You should be thankful for that."

Harriet punched Freddy, which made her feel a little happier! As Freddy was lying on the ground, Jenny, Mickey and Harriet surrounded him. Each took it in turns to speak to Freddy Fixer.

"I didn't want you to fix anything, Freddy. I just wanted you to listen to me, maybe ask me about my grandmother, ask if you could do anything," said Jenny.

"I didn't want you to fix anything, Freddy. I just wanted you to sit with me and maybe listen to me tell you how I was feeling, maybe remember some fun stories of me and my dog," said Mickey.

"I didn't want you to fix anything, Freddy. I just wanted you to tell me you cared, and you would help me get through it," said Harriet.

The moral of the story is simple: you do not always have to fix anything… and duck when Harriet looks angry!

Global Story – Dale Carnegie Influences a Dinner Guest

Dale Carnegie was renowned for being able to make friends and influence people, be that in social or business settings. His book, *How to Win Friends and Influence People*, first published in 1936, was the first of many to be published and global sales to date are in the tens of millions. He was very observant of others' words, moods, expressions, body language, social and business distance, social collaborations, and observed professional demeanour. His work, although it is now old, is still relevant. Here is a story I read about ten years ago.

Dale Carnegie was invited to a very highbrow formal dinner evening which was being hosted by a business executive. The host had invited many of his work colleagues, and some of his chosen friends, who were equally successful in their own fields. Several people were sitting around a large oval table and at the head was the host. After the starter course, and while everyone was waiting for the main course, the host started to recount a story about a certain author and how he came to create his stories.

As the story progressed, everyone was listening intently. As a funny anecdote was shared, everyone laughed appropriately with the host. Then a young man stood up and said:

"Excuse me, but I think you will find that story was pinched from another writer – your author did not originally say that!"

Everyone went quiet, not knowing who to believe, but also feeling a little embarrassed that the host had been challenged so formally. He was angry, dismissed the claim outright, and carried on with his story.

Afterwards, Dale Carnegie took the person to one side who had interrupted and publicly challenged the host:

"Maybe you had the correct dates, maybe you didn't. That is not the point. If your motive were to embarrass the host with your 'knowledge' then you succeeded one hundred per cent. But would it not have been a better idea to hold your tongue while he was speaking? Then afterwards, if your curiosity got the better of you, why didn't you say, 'I loved your story, but never knew his birth and death dates were what you mentioned, I had heard something different... but still, a great story'."

The man looked at Dale Carnegie and did not need to say a word. His face did that for him. Dale Carnegie had put him in his place and made him thankful in the process which was an art in itself! (Dale Carnegie, 2019).

What would you have done if you were in the place of Dale Carnegie at the dinner table?

Carnegie sums up this type of emotional awareness in business by the following three sentences:

- *Always give more than expected.*
- *Always give more than you take.*
- *Never give an opinion unless asked.*

However, this emotional awareness is only part of emotional intelligence. Emotional intelligence is the ability to perceive, interpret, demonstrate, control, evaluate, and use emotions to communicate with and relate to others effectively and constructively (Verywell Mind, 2023).

In simple terms this means to be aware of other people's needs, moods, and situations, and then act accordingly. When linked with empathy, which is the ability to feel someone else's situation, be with someone, rather than feel for them, as in pity, then we start to possess emotional intelligence.

The Accountant Uses the Elephant

Chip and Dan Heath (2011) have been modern-day exponents of using emotional intelligence to get results, especially when a rational approach to a challenge does not work. They coin the phrase 'the Elephant and the Rider' which refers to the prefrontal cortex of the brain being very rational, aka the Rider. The Rider makes all the rational decisions and often controls the emotional limbic system, aka the Elephant.

If we want to succeed in life we will surely need to be rational. Yet there are occasions where being rational is ineffective. This is especially true when our emotional limbic system kicks in. This is where the Elephant takes charge, and in effect, can override the Rider.

Chip and Dan Heath use a sublime example of this when they recount the story of the accounts executive who was presenting to his seniors in the boardroom. He had shown his seniors the bottom-line account that stated, in black and white, that the company was losing significant amounts of money buying gloves from one particular supplier.

Many of these gloves were of poor quality, and often needed to be replaced quickly, at more cost. Still, his rational monologue was going unheard until he switched tack and appealed to the emotions of the seniors by employing the Elephant. He proceeded to throw a pair of gloves on the table every few seconds whilst telling the seniors this was the amount of wastage that was happening, literally as they spoke. Within a few moments, with countless pairs of gloves littering the table, the seniors had a change of mind!

If you want to succeed in any aspect of life, you may well have to employ the emotional Elephant.

Sarah's Emotional Coffee

To give a bit of a modern twist and balance to emotional intelligence, here is a story about somebody who displayed incredible emotional intelligence.

Sarah Willingham, CEO of hospitality group Nightcap (and former Dragon on the TV show *Dragon's Den*) suffered from 'imposter syndrome' where she felt not good enough professionally. In a previous position, she describes the feeling of being overwhelmed and how she responded in a way that demonstrated great emotional confidence, but also banished her imposter syndrome for good.

She was two minutes late for a meeting. The person on the opposite side of the boardroom table, a lawyer, looked up and said:

"Thank goodness, mine's a white with one sugar please."

Sarah did not react verbally, or show any different emotion, but rather, walked calmly round the table to get a coffee, thinking over what had just happened. She made him the coffee, put it in front of him, and asked if anybody else would like a coffee. Sarah made herself a coffee and sat back down again opposite him. As he looked up, Sarah watched the colour drain from his face as he realised the enormous assumption he had made.

It was such a beautiful empowering moment in Sarah's career as she sat there and realised she had been completely misjudged, but had responded with emotional intelligence. The imposter syndrome she thought she had, was now a superpower quality (Sarah Willingham – *BBC Business News*, 2022).

Guess who walked out of that boardroom with the deal?

Emotional intelligence and empathy can be difficult concepts to understand, and certainly difficult to interpret and display. Often it seems that some people are better at this than others. While I agree with this, it may be that once you are aware of the importance of emotional intelligence and empathy, you can start to use it and maximise its benefits.

Do you employ emotional intelligence and empathy at work and with friends and family? If not, what is stopping you?

My Story – The New Teachers on the Block

Over the years I have worked with many diverse groups. However, one group I really enjoyed working with was young professionals, be they university undergraduates, National Citizenship Service students or early career teachers (ECT) cohorts. The reason for this is that they generally don't have rigid views, and so are open to different approaches and are keen to learn. As such, they usually engage with my interactive learning.

I was once delivering a session to twelve ECT students in Haslingden. The workshop was on Growth Mindset and how to merge this seamlessly into Teaching Principles in the classroom. We went over the concepts of Growth Mindset, and then used some interactive exercises to show how this worked in the classroom, around the school and with parents.

I started to bridge the gap into Teaching Principles, talking about differentiation, group work benefits versus losses, subject safety and security of pupils, seating arrangements, and classroom layout. We then went next door where we had several pupils ready to be taught and here the ECT students could put this new knowledge and philosophy into practice.

What struck me was almost all of the students were well-organised, had the knowledge and had picked up the basic taught principles and were applying them. However, what was also clearly apparent was the inability of many students to grasp the emotional connection with pupils. It was as if they were robots, imparting the knowledge, setting up groups, recording learning outcomes, praising pupils and then moving on to the next topic.

The teaching was being done *to* the pupils, rather than being done *with* the pupils. There was a clear lack of empathy for learners, with both those who progressed quickly, and those who encountered problems. They were not carrying the pupils along emotionally. They rarely listened fully to the pupils and were often caught interrupting them. I wanted them to listen to understand, not listen to interrupt.

This robotic, albeit technically correct teaching, might look good for learning outcomes, and even Ofsted, but pupil engagement will suffer. If there is any consolation to the ECT students, I have also witnessed this empathy disconnect with senior leadership teams (SLT's) in schools.

These SLT's are much more knowledgeable in their professional remit than me, but they too could be seen as robots dropping knowledge bites, giving didactic advice to pupils, or administering sanctions. This was often done without an emotional connection. Maybe this was due to their lack of time, but I suspect there was more to it than that.

Similarly, I was invited to watch Year 7, 8 and 9 (ages eleven to fourteen) in a debate presentation final between several schools. Without question, many of the speakers were organised, knew their stuff, and had logical arguments and themes. But I wasn't engaged with the process.

Why wasn't I fully engaged?

The answer was clear: some spoke a little too fast which left little time to digest and process the information. But, crucially, I do not remember one speaker who actually fully engaged with the audience. Rather they spilt out their knowledge *at* the audience. They were not working *with* the audience. There was no tangible empathy of checking responses, reactions, or even facial expressions. All the pupils were probably too polished with no emotional connection to the audience. Nevertheless, they were still excellent, and very brave, given their age.

Tim Gallwey Lets Them learn

I was reminded of this lack of empathy in coaching when I attended an online seminar with the celebrated coach, Tim Gallwey, who was responsible for the highly acclaimed and successful book series *The Inner Game*. On this seminar were around two hundred and fifty people, all waiting for the inside track of the secrets to getting the right mindset in coaching.

He went through various models of performance, which was fine, and told a few anecdotes with name drops. But then he mentioned his pet hate:

"When I am working with younger people, and they are learning the basics of a tennis shot, maybe for the first time, I don't overload them. I let them learn. So often I see people over-coaching and this approach stunts the ability of the child to try for themselves, to make their own mistakes, to learn their own way of playing and solving challenges. Let them learn and then get into dialogue about what worked and didn't work... now that's real coaching and real empathy!"

This was brilliant. Keep it simple, give them time and space, but empathetically engage with the learner along *their* learning process.

I don't think the two younger co-hosts really understood this, as they seemed to be constantly interrupting Tim during many parts of the webinar!

⟨?⟩ *Have you ever interrupted a learning process too soon or too often?*

Deep Dive – Empathetic Communication – Face it, Dr Ekman

Paul Ekman is an American psychologist and professor emeritus at the University of California, San Francisco. He is a pioneer in the study of emotions and their relationship to facial expressions. In effect, he has devised a system to read people (Paul Ekman.com).

He talks about the seven basic human facial expressions of *happiness, surprise, anger, sadness, fear, contempt and disgust.* He has worked out that there are thousands of micro facial expressions humans can make when they demonstrate any of the seven basic emotions. This makes reading somebody very complex, and by that nature, extremely difficult, especially when these expressions can mean different things in different cultures. However, Dr Ekman reads these micro expressions and is much sought after in the law enforcement, and on various TV shows, like Fox Network's *Lie to Me* as he predicts emotions and behaviours (Wikipedia, Paul Ekman).

I have used a series of Dr Ekman's images, of people with different expressions, and given these to students and delegates, and asked them to tell me which of the seven facial expressions are being made. More often than not, it was the females in the group that consistently scored higher than the males.

What makes this process more difficult is that humans have around eighty-seven different emotions and feelings according to Dr Brené Brown, and some commentators say there are many more than this. If we add into this the different types of body language, then the whole process of understanding someone, with faces and emotions, beyond their words, becomes fraught with misinterpretation.

Deep Dive – Empathetic Active Listening – Hear the Tumbleweed

I learnt much of my active listening in three settings:

1. Working with challenged young adults who had strong emotions and volatile behaviours, especially if you did not engage empathetically with them.
2. As a mental health trainer with MHFA England and my own in-house courses, delivering hundreds of courses on empathetic active listening. This was more of a challenge as half of these courses were online.
3. From third party accounts and my reading of Samaritans literature including Katie Colombus (2021).

Very quickly I realised that this was a skill that could not only help with listening conversations, but it could be adapted for use in many management positions.

So, what is Empathetic Active Listening?

On a basic level, this means being authentically interested in and listening to what somebody else is saying with a view to understanding them, exploring options, supporting them and validating their views.

Simply, it is listening to understand, without judgement, so that the person being supported can feel valued and comfortable in articulating the full nature of their situation. This may also involve periods of silence as the person thinks through their challenge – Tumbleweed Time.

It may also involve validating and reassuring the person, summarising their thoughts and feelings and checking with the person that the listener has really understood what has been shared. All of this should be done with compassion.

If conducted well, this process will engender trust on both sides, which may well solicit further unravelling of thoughts and emotions. Sometimes these thoughts and feelings may be so well hidden that the person themself doesn't even know they exist. A good active listener can help the talker uncover these things, like picking up a stone at the beach and finding an unexpected crustacean underneath.

Ultimately the person being supported may start to take more ownership of their situation and this may result in them instigating positive changes. A feeling of clarity may emerge from a previous place of insecurity and chaos, almost like a decluttering of an untidy room. A good listener therefore empowers the talker.

If the listener can make the person being supported feel like the most important in the world, that each and every word and emotion is valuable and almost sacred, then anything is possible.

If the listener can weave hope and the prospect of recovery into the process then this is always a great foundation on which to base the relationship.

If you're a manager or a leader, your progress will be stunted if you do not possess active empathetic listening skills.

What does this not involve?

Trying to fix a situation, listening to interrupt, giving advice, being judgemental and being in a rush! Even putting your own 'spin' on what has been shared. When we try and fix it automatically, it's all about you, the listener, and this takes away the ability of the talker to self-solve.

It also does not mean 'hijacking' someone's thoughts with your own opinions and experiences. There may be a place for this sharing of personal experiences, but certainly not in the early stages of understanding and supporting the person. Perhaps involving an independent third-party example of someone else who encountered something similar might be the way to go in the first instance... but not in the early stages.

Here is an example of poor empathy and hijacking from a visit to an independent consultant recently about my knee problems:

Ross: "After the operation my knee hurts in different places and it's worse than before."

Doctor: "We have all got things wrong with our bodies. My knees are not the same now and I can't play squash the way I used to!"

Wow! Not only was he saying that I just have to suck it up and get on with it, but he also tried to liken his discomfort and activity, to my pain and inactivity. A classic case of hijacking that tries to make you feel guilty.

A better response would have been:

"Wow, that must be difficult. Tell me more about this?"

Or he could just have employed silence with a few nods, which would have given me tacit permission to carry on and elaborate about my situation and my feelings.

Have you ever hijacked somebody, and could the outcome have been better if you hadn't employed this tactic?

Sometimes, we perceive the more successful people amongst us as those perhaps being louder and more direct. However, before you get to this place, try some soft emotional intelligence and empathetic listening. It goes so much further than you think, and more often than not, it just involves being interested and listening to the person.

Celebrity examples of this are Mark Zuckerberg, founder of Facebook. He even won an award for 'world-class listening' and Richard Branson who said, "Listen more than you talk."

Deep Dive – Direct Communication – Desperately Seeking Susan for a Fierce Conversation

I came across Susan Scott (*Fierce Conversations*, 2003) around twelve years ago when another coach recommended her book to me. I have used it extensively since and I am going to distil her key questions further below.

Her premise is that when we communicate, we often avoid conflict or confrontation. Yet it is this very conflict or confrontation that needs addressing… sometimes. I like this approach, but I am still a dedicated advocate of an initial listening and empathy approach.

Here are her distilled six questions you might need to ask somebody if you want to resolve an issue:

1. I would like to talk about X (nice confrontation).
2. I would like to hear your perspective about X (empathy).
3. I would like to share my perspective about X (empathy).
4. Together, I know we can work this out as we are on the same side, and we will take as long as it takes (shared empathy).
5. We both have something to lose, but more to gain (shared empathy).
6. At the end of the day, it is about the client/child who comes first (shared empathy).

This approach might not be for everyone, and seems to go against our premise of adopting empathy. Yet sometimes, if direct communication is done with empathy, it might just be exactly what is needed.

Deep Dive – Direct Communication – Julie Heads for Some Good Solutions

Julie Cole, an experienced primary school headteacher, Ofsted inspector and friend, is someone who really sums up Lesson 6 on emotional intelligence, active empathetic listening and direct communication.

When I first met Julie a few years ago, it was evident she had many professional and personal qualities that made her an effective educator and an engaging person. What I have since learnt is that Julie can approach challenges in different ways according to what she thinks will work out best.

For example, she is not averse to gently questioning any staff member about something with a view to quickly getting them to see if there is a better way to resolve a challenge. When a senior staff member had opened the school gates too early, allowing pupils to enter the dining hall before the food was ready, she was swift to act by asking if the said staff member could assist in the dining room as the food wasn't ready yet. The next day, the school gates were opened on time and not before time.

Equally she is a competent proponent of Susan Scott's direct communication and I have witnessed this with some parents. She lets the parent talk, validates their feelings, but often produces evidence to back up her viewpoint. I suspect many parents secretly admire this approach as they know where they stand and are listened to.

However, I feel her best quality is that she can use a variety of bespoke responses to match a challenge. Sometimes she will look at a challenge in a completely different way to me, often with a good degree of patience, and at other times she will get me to reflect on my own feelings and attitude and this helps me get things in perspective.

Deep Dive – Blended Approach – 'Parky' Knows Best

Perhaps a really good example of this blend of empathy and direct communication was witnessed with the late Sir Michael Parkinson as he hosted his legendary TV chat shows over many years. Since the start of his debut with the BBC in 1971 until 2007, he spoke to two thousand guests, in 650 shows over thirty-six years, often pulling in TV audiences of over twelve million viewers (*BBC News*, 2023).

Many of the guests were global icons such as film director Orson Welles, boxer Muhammad Ali, actor Bette Davis, actor/singer/dancer Fred Astaire and philosopher Jacob Bronowski.

Many observers saw him as the consummate interviewer for several reasons:

- He did thorough research on each guest.
- Was passionately interested and curious in his guests (partly because he had a big say in who was interviewed).
- He was not afraid of asking direct or even personal questions.
- He listened for longer periods of the interview than he talked.
- He was not afraid to ditch the scripted questions (as was the case when interviewing Orson Welles).

Sir Richard Attenborough complimented his research. He said that 'Parky' asked questions that he had never thought of, and it made him delve inside himself introspectively to reveal insightful thoughts which were then discussed.

Crucially, Parky gave him the time to think. He gave him Tumbleweed.

Interestingly, when Parky had big personalities on the show, such as Billy Connolly, he made sure the other guests were not dwarfed or left out of the interview process – excellent emotional awareness. However, his approach was not without incident, as was the case on two occasions in particular when he asked direct, personal questions.

Once in the seventies, at the start of the femininity movement, he pointedly asked actor Helen Mirren if her 'equipment' ever got in the way of her being taken seriously. This was not received well, and maybe today's social media might have cast him aside? Secondly, in 2003, he asked actor Meg Ryan some very direct questions about her that she took offence to, so she replied only in short sentences:

"Are you wary of journalists… since you trained to be one?"

Meg Ryan replied, "What do you mean?"

Parky carried on with the theme and stopped her replying by asking another question:

"I can tell you're wary of me now, and the way you are sitting tells me that you're wary… if you were me now, what would you do?"

"I would wrap it up!" she replied curtly.

It was probably not the response he was looking for and it goes to show that being direct for too long can offend people. Overall, he was lauded for his skillset. This acclaim did not happen overnight, in fact it took many years, with a few hiccups.

But being aware of the needs of others and being direct on occasions eventually gave him global accreditation.

After his death his son Mike revealed that Parky suffered from imposter syndrome and was in awe of his TV bosses and many of his guests, probably in part as a result of his working-class background.

A final example of a lack of empathy and connection was demonstrated to me recently when I had my post-operative meeting with my knee surgeon. It was only three months post-op from my total knee replacement. I was experiencing a distressing clunking of my knee which made driving very uncomfortable. I could not cycle, and I still had a partly numb foot.

As I limped into his consulting room, I detected a frostiness to his manner. It was beyond his normal, direct, no-nonsense approach which I quite liked and was the reason I chose him in the first place. He did not examine my knee. He did not get out of his chair, and he did not even shake my hand. Rather, he told me bluntly that recovery can vary, and he would see me in a year. The whole experience lasted less than two minutes.

This is an excellent example of a non-model of empathy, i.e. not making any effort to connect with my emotions, an experience on his part, devoid of any real empathy.

I may yet make more recovery, and he may well be right, but what I was looking for in that very moment was empathy, especially as I had waited nearly thirty-nine years for a new knee. I wanted him to gently reassure me, and take a sincere interest in what I was saying.

Have you ever experienced a situation like this, or even instigated one?

On a lighter note, when I was recently visiting Wrightington Hospital for an ankle injection, I happened to engage with a very friendly nurse. As is my trademark, whenever I am with medical experts I always have a few questions I want answering and this situation was no different. I was looking for some inside knowledge and maybe some empathy. The conversation went something like this:

Ross: "I know I am here for my ankle injection, but I have atrial fibrillation. Sometimes I wonder if my stomach gets so upset that it causes the atrial fibrillation or could it be that the atrial fibrillation causes my upset stomach?"

Nurse: "Yes."

This demonstrated one simple thing... she wasn't really listening and the rapport we had just developed, disappeared instantly.

Famous Example of Emotional Intelligence – We Can't Hear Mr Broon

When I was working at PNEFC with Craig Brown (ex-national team manager of Scotland), he had an engaging manner and was the epitome of emotional intelligence, and in particular was an astonishing empathetic listener.

During my first ever conversation with him, it immediately struck me how interested he was in what I had to say. He never interrupted me, kept smiling, nodding, and where appropriate, asked questions. At the end of the conversation, I thanked him for his time and interest. What he said next has stuck with me ever since:

"No, thank you, Ross, it really was my pleasure to understand more about you and the important role you play."

It was not just what he said, but it was also the way he meant every single word.

"*You can make more friends in two months by becoming interested in other people than you can in two years by trying to get other people interested in you.*" Dale Carnegie (1888–1955) author, self-improvement course writer, international speaker.

SONOMA Waypoint Wisdom 45:

In life, we try to fix things and more often than not, we just want to be listened to, be understood, to be cared for and even loved.

SONOMA Waypoint Wisdom 46:

First-level emotional intelligence is being aware of the needs of people. When this is linked to empathy, we are then able to fully respond to situations and environments. It's about understanding and relating to the needs of others.

SONOMA Waypoint Wisdom 47:

Let people learn, give them time and space with minimal feedback initially. But always be present empathetically to their learning needs in this process.

SONOMA Waypoint Wisdom 48:

To empathetically support someone, try and listen to understand, rather than listen to interrupt. Engage by active listening of nods and small linking words. Give them time to fully empty their thoughts by using Tumbleweed moments. Summarise thoughts where appropriate without judging responses.

SONOMA *Waypoint Wisdom* **49:**

A final thought on an accepted aphorism:

"Treat people as you would like to be treated" maybe should read, *"Treat people as* they *would like to be treated."*

QR Code Express Conversations & Mind Exercises into...
Active Empathetic Listening

Measure your performance and add scores to the PSCP Matrix at the end of the book

Personal Sonoma Colour Profile –
6: Measurement of Emotional Intelligence & Empathetic Listening

Answer each question honestly.

Answer Always, Sometimes or Never

1. I can recognise my emotions when I am experiencing them.
2. I can be in tune to other people's emotions.
3. I am aware of my communication strengths and weaknesses.
4. I am aware of how others might be feeling by their facial expressions.
5. I am able to fully listen and engage with others to try to understand them.
6. I am authentically interested in the welfare of others.
7. I check in with people.
8. I know when to discuss my feelings with others.
9. I know how to calm myself down when I am upset.
10. I can adapt my style to meet the needs of others.
11. I can listen to understand, rather than listen to interrupt.
12. I can feel comfortable with silence when I am supporting someone else.

Scoring

Always = 3 points, Sometimes = 2 points, Never = 1 point

Sonoma Gold = 25-36

You are very much aware of other people's feelings and emotions and can take appropriate action to soothe and resolve a situation. You have very good self-awareness of emotions and behaviours.

Sonoma Silver = 13-24

You have some awareness of other people's feelings and emotions and can sometimes take appropriate action to soothe and resolve a situation. You have an awareness of your own emotions and behaviours, but may need to review these.

Sonoma Bronze = 1-12

You have a limited awareness of other people's feelings and emotions and occasionally can take appropriate action to soothe and resolve a situation. You have a limited awareness of personal emotions and behaviours, and these need to be changed.

Summary of Summer

The tide is in and it's waiting for you. Like you, it is impatient to start its journey with you. Everything is possible and the speed and depth of the tide takes your breath away. It is a rollercoaster of adventure that will hopefully bring you your just desserts.

It's a time to stretch your legs and expand your mind, take some chances and risks. Opportunities abound and life has boundless possibilities. You might not know it, but this delightful whirlwind of a journey, high on the ocean waves has a time limit. You must maximise every opportunity.

Summer is also a time to enjoy the fruits of your labour. To bask in your new status, congratulate yourself, but do not rest on your laurels for too long. This Season can quickly turn into borrowed time and in the distance the Autumn is beckoning maybe with more opportunities.

But it might also be the Season that starts to drag you down beneath the waves. But still, keep your youthful approach, ride the waves and trust in the process of life and expectation of the forthcoming Season.

"Summer's lease hath all too short a date." William Shakespeare (1564–1616) English playwright and poet.

Autumn

Autumn is a time to consolidate the fruits of our labours and reflect on where we are in our career. We start to fully understand the future direction to take in life. We could be entering a period of significant change, and for some this change could be the start of an evergreen period, while for others, this change may be the start of a period of calm acceptance or even decline.

As the crops are being harvested we can assess our existing skills, knowledge and experience. How we proceed depends on what we want and need for ourselves and those we care about.

Specifically, on your Sonoma journey, it is a time to:

- Enhance your performance levels with a calm and focused eye.
- Seek out opportunities for collaboration and connection.
- Learn that vulnerability and self-compassion could be valuable allies.
- Understand the value of altruism and philanthropy.
- Maintain clarity and reliability, whilst being watchful of procrastination.

- Manage your physical, emotional and mental states.
- Encounter change in the form of career, life and health.

Our garden which has been in full bloom, may start to wither and fade unless we remain open to lessons which could still have a qualitative and quantitative impact upon our lives.

"Autumn carries more gold in its pocket than all the other seasons." Jim Bishop (1907–1987) American journalist and author.

Lesson 7:

Late Bloomers & Unexpected Early Wilters

Performance, Visualisation, Connectivity, Collaboration & Vulnerability

Hidden Story – The Sting in the Tale

Male or drone honeybees' sole purpose in life is to fertilise the Queen bee. To this end, each bee has to sufficiently entertain the Queen before the victor can mate with her. Unfortunately, the winning bee will die shortly afterwards as his reproductive organ is ripped out after mating, and the worker bees refuse to feed him as he has served his role in the hive.

Each bee sets about practising their song and dance routines until there are two bees left. One of them is a natural, with all the right moves and a voice which is pitch perfect. He is the favourite to win after several days of heats. But the Queen, who is old and seen the ritual many times before, has developed a soft spot for the other finalist. He, whilst talented, is more hesitant and afraid of making a fool of himself. He becomes consumed by the prospect of failure.

The first bee introduces himself confidently and performs his song and dance routine:

"Honeybee mine, together we can shine, tomorrow we can be wed, and then I will be dead."

The Queen cannot deny he is impressive and consults with her workers. Unanimously they award him 9/10. His song was a cover of a hit by the Honeycombs.

The second bee is nervous and worried that he will forget his routine and has never performed his self-composed song in public before. He knows it is a huge risk and that if he loses he will be banished from the hive. He is tentative and as he is about to sing, he forgets his words. A silence cascades throughout the apiary. The Queen just about manages to contain her disappointment and sadness for her favourite as everyone starts to laugh loudly. The score is 0/10. A complete failure and he is banished to end his short life all alone.

A few days pass, and a worker bee spots the losing bee, whose failure is now legendary amongst his colleagues. He offers him a proposition. The worker bee is willing to help him overcome his nerves and secure him another entry in the next series of mating heats.

In return, the loser bee must promote the upcoming event to all his friends that are still in contact with him from the hives. The worker bee will benefit from receiving all the proceeds.

The losing bee accepts and gets posters printed for the event. He does a few PR stunts that the worker bee set up for him – an interview on Buzz Radio and a live singing and dancing appearance on the BBC's *Be Scene Today* programme.

The day before the first heat, the losing bee asks the worker bee:

"Hey, I have done what you have asked and fulfilled my part of the bargain. When are you going to teach me how to calm my nerves so I can win the Queen over?"

The worker bee replies very calmly and slowly:

"But I have been teaching you. I put my trust in you by supporting you and I set up media opportunities for you to meet people, to let them see and hear you sing and dance. In return you forgot about your nerves. Your passion for the event rose above your nervousness. You are now ready to perform in front of the Queen. Now it is as an opportunity rather than a threat."

Sure enough, the losing bee does feel better and less anxious. But he still has doubts waiting in the wings and misses his cue to start. His music intro begins, and he flies to centre stage and sings and dances his heart out. The audience love it and give him a flying ovation. But the old Queen is still and silent – she has died. All the years of waiting and the euphoria of expectation at finally mating with someone she really liked has given her a heart attack.

Perhaps the moral of the story is threefold:

1. Believe in yourself.
2. Get others to believe in you and support you.
3. Take the opportunity when it comes as it might not come around again.

Global Story – Phelps, Watson & Macpherson Can See the End in Mind

World-famous champion swimmer Michael Phelps has twenty-three Olympic gold medals. As an eleven-year-old his potential was evident and top swimming coach Bob Bowman was enlisted as his official coach. Over the years, progress and success were gradual. Phelps had a physique perfectly suited to swimming but was obsessive in many of his behaviours. He did not have the right routines consistently around diet, sleep, training, rest, and almost seemed random in his approach to swimming. He was soon diagnosed with ADHD which was why he had difficulty with his focus and concentration.

Stories of Bowman using visualisation are almost legendary. Last thing at night, and first thing in the morning, Phelps would relax his body and mind before visualising his whole race, i.e. dive start, every stroke, turn and finish. Bowman encouraged him to study video footage to track what he had envisaged matched reality. Once these core routines were put in place, they could start working on other aspects of his preparation.

This breaking down of component parts, analysing these small wins, or marginal gains, were the key to his future success. Before a race the dawn and dusk visualisation techniques coincided with Phelps putting on his headphones as he thought about each specific part of the race ahead. Even when his goggles occasionally failed, he just visualised overcoming this with calmness.

"When I would visualise," Phelps says. "It would be what you want it to be, what you don't want it to be, what it could be. You are always ready for whatever comes your way."

Anthony Watson is another athlete who uses performance and visualisation techniques. He is an England rugby player who uses sports performance and visualisation expert Don Macpherson. Together they visualise specific try-scoring moments on the pitch and go through them in microscopic details in terms of technical skill, emotional feeling, position on the pitch, the actual moment of scoring the try and even celebrating afterwards.

Speaking with Don, it is clear that he understands the power of the subconscious mind and has worked his magic with elite athletes such as Pat Cash, George Ford, Damon Hill, et al. In particular, he sagaciously identifies the area of neuroscience as the key to understanding and developing mindset, and ipso facto, positive visualisation power and capacity potential.

Interestingly, Arnold Schwarzenegger once quoted him:

"*What you can see, you can be, as the sports psychologist Don Macpherson has famously said.*"
Arnold Schwarzenegger, author of *Be Useful, Seven Tools for Life*.

Now, if Arnie believes in Don and visualisation belief, then they must be onto something!

There are many sports psychologists, coaches, football managers and athlete mentors like Phelps, Bowman, Watson and Mcpherson who use visualisation as a technique to deal with potential disasters. This often involves visualising what could go wrong in performance then searching for an image and feeling of dealing with it, like preprogramming to deal with the 'if and when' scenarios. When all the senses and angles to performance are vividly imagined, the positive results usually follow.

A simple example of this are coaches and managers who rehearse going behind in a match even before the game starts.

My Story – Opportunity Knocks

My first large-scale public presentation was in front of fifteen thousand fans at Preston North End FC, in 1995. I had hosted and talked at many public events before, in Saudi Arabia, Canada, USA and at various UK conferences. But this happened unexpectedly and involved bigger numbers than I had previously experienced.

At the time, I was working at Preston College as a PE lecturer, and was attending the match socially at the football club's home ground. As half-time approached, I heard that the regular half-time pitch-side announcer had been taken ill and the club secretary was desperately searching for a replacement. I have no explanation as to what came over me, but I went across to the directors' box and offered my services. What made my case irresistible was the fact I was known to the management, and nobody else had volunteered!

I grabbed the microphone and practised my script just before half-time. I would not describe myself as nervous, rather, I wanted to do a good job and I would not have been able to live with myself afterwards if I had been struck by nerves and made a hash of things. Without knowing it, this strategy of thinking forward, or visualising, was the way I motivated myself.

With microphone in hand on the pitch, I proceeded to call out the lottery winners, interview a former player and had just enough time to conduct a mini-penalty shoot-out competition.

There were no major disasters, which was a relief, and the thrill of 'holding public court' was like an addiction and I wanted more. After the match, I was asked to be standby again, and within a few months, I was promoted to regular announcer. In the next year, I was offered a full-time job at the club which was to last five years. Not bad for volunteering to speak on the pitch one Saturday afternoon!

Have you ever been in a situation like this, and it all turned out well in the end?

Tony is in the Building

Many years later, after many public speaking gigs at education and business conferences, I was 'recognised' at an event I was about to speak at. A middle-aged lady leading a small group of people approached me. The conversation went something like this:

"We love your work. We have seen you all over the UK and think you're amazing! You do seem bigger close up though!"

My head started to swell, and I played with the thought that maybe I had finally made it. I also started to think what she meant when she said I was bigger close up. Before I could let my imagination run further away, she was talking to me again:

"I am with all my family, and I didn't think you were advertised to speak here today – this is such a surprise. I do hope it's as good as the Radisson Blu gig you did in London?"

I was stopped dead in my tracks. My mind was racing. I had talked in London, but never at the Radisson Blu… ever!

The conversation and the confusion continued:

"Would you mind signing your book? I always take it with me everywhere I go."

Before I could reply she pulled out *Awaken the Giant Within*, an international best-seller book written by celebrated author and speaker Tony Robbins!

Yes, we are both speakers, yes, we are both quite tall with a heavy build, and yes, we are similar in age (Tony is a year older than me). But he is known around the world, he is super rich, and he has an American accent… I have none of those attributes!

Somewhere in my head I am quickly weighing up the alternatives:

1. Do I confess that I am not Tony Robbins, and in doing so, spoil her experience and cause her embarrassment in front of her family?
2. Do I just sign the book, make her happy and hope our paths never cross again?

She passed me a pen and my mind was made up.

I scribbled something that resembled a child's first writing experience, and by doing so, made sure it was anything but legible.

If I thought this was the end of the encounter, then I was severely mistaken:

"Can we have a selfie with you too… *Tony*?"

A crime had already been committed so what had I left to lose?

I stood in the middle of the group and smiled. With selfie and book in hand, they wished me well and waved goodbye. I allowed myself a little internal chuckle. But then I realised the error of my decision to impersonate Tony Robbins… I still had to speak at the gig!

Twenty minutes later I was introduced on stage. I looked around the audience and to my horror, sat two rows back from the front was my new number one fan. Our eyes met briefly, and her face was a picture of bemusement, followed by immediate embarrassment.

Deep Dive – Performance

Often when I have been attending corporate or senior leadership team meetings, I have come across poor, nervous speaking performances. This could be down to what we touched on in Lesson 5 about imposter syndrome where somebody feels they are not good enough, especially when they are talking to their peers.

More often than not, the person is either:

- Speaking too fast, which can present problems for the audience understanding the message, and it can stop the speaker thinking clearly.

- They are meandering and not getting to the point.
- They are trying to be funny when they are clearly not.

It could be that the speaker has not set the scene correctly or has not identified the problem before presenting the audience with a solution.

All of these errors prevent listeners from fully processing information.

I witnessed this first hand at a large comprehensive school in Manchester in 2018. The Assistant Head was stuttering when talking to me before he addressed the crowd of one hundred or so fellow teachers. He then looked at me and said:

"Any tips to help me calm down?"

I asked him if he was considering going for Headship in the future. He replied that he had thought about it and had all the right background knowledge to be a successful Head, but had this mental block about public speaking. I had put his aspirations back to the forefront of his mind.

I then told him that public speaking is a learnt habit, and the more times you practise the better you generally become... but time was short!

I decided to offer to speak with him. I would do a quick introduction, he would thank staff for attending, then hand back to me briefly to go over the agenda. This gave him time to catch his breath, and crucially, practise a calming technique of anchoring his thumb and finger together whilst imagining a great outcome.

Then I asked him to say to himself:

No need to get nervous, this crowd is not a threat, I want to be here and it's all going to go well.

Without him knowing it, this technique of affirmations and anchoring speaks to the subconscious mind. It says the room and people are not a threat. This is an opportunity on the road to Headship.

With a few techniques, and a sharing of the spotlight, where attention is split, both parties can perform better.

Guess what? It went okay. The next time it went better, and eventually he became a super high-flying Head.

The subconscious mind has so much to do with public performance and we are going to examine this further.

Deep Dive – Performance – Dr Yeung is Never Wrong

Some form of performance is inevitable if you want to be accredited in life. Whether it is in front of fifteen thousand people, one hundred peers, within a team of office professionals, or even your social peers.

I believe performance in all aspects of life is initially a learnt habit. We are not born as natural performers or speakers, but rather, we learn along the way. Planning and preparation around performance helps this process. Equally, rituals and routines, especially what we do first to make us feel safe before we perform, helps us to feel secure.

Examples of this are getting to the venue early, checking resources and IT, memorising delegate names and maybe a toilet visit before you start. When preparation is tied in with motivation, desire, opportunity, practice, support, and feedback, then progress becomes self-evident.

In public speaking for example, eminent psychologist and business speaker, Dr Rob Yeung (2008), talks about our nerves and turning these into needs. For example, when you first start speaking in public, you might be nervous. Over time, with guidance and practice you can turn the nerves into enjoyment. Even your perceived failures (which generally are not as bad as what we think) are stepping stones to mastery and enjoyment of public speaking.

From my own experience, when I began to enjoy public speaking, I then needed the regular high of engaging with an audience. This is the place most accomplished speakers get to. So, when people ask if you are nervous, this becomes a redundant question. I have heard athletes speak about being adrenalised, which is probably a better way of putting things. Maybe we can say we are 'optimally adrenalised'.

What are some of the theoretical and practical processes that have helped you in live public performance?

Hippo & Amy – Use Them or Let Them Destroy You

It all starts with the limbic system in the brain, and specifically our friends Hippo and Amy, the hippocampus and the amygdala which we mentioned in Lesson 4.

The hippocampus as we have previously seen, has several functions which revolve around memory formation and storage, emotions and learning. Crucially, it works best when it is motivated. Therefore, in a simple example, if you are not that bothered about passing an exam, it does not form, store and retrieve information as effectively. This can be problematic.

The amygdala is primarily concerned with emotions, especially fear, anxiety and aggression. When we perceive fear for example, it sends messages to the adrenal cortex in the kidneys to release the stress hormones adrenaline and cortisol which are there to regulate our feelings and emotions.

However, a too rapid response and an overproduction of these hormones instantaneously flood the prefrontal cortex which impact the ability to be rational and make decisions – like a rabbit in the headlights scenario. When this happens, we can become a jabbering wreck – this is known as the 'amygdala hijack'.

Often this is what is happening when we experience a panic attack. We do not think straight, we hyperventilate and we catastrophise. I should know as I have had over fifty of these episodes.

So how do we prevent this from happening?

The first part is to have a rational awareness. If we are about to perform, or have started to perform, and we feel this 'rabbit in the headlights' scenario, then apply logic by being aware of it. Your body has over-prepared you for the task and released too much adrenaline and cortisol.

Secondly, begin slow deep breathing, to dilute this impact, slowing the heart rate, and reduce the exit of carbon dioxide from the lungs. It compares with instances of hyperventilation; we excrete too much carbon dioxide too quickly which can make us feel light-headed. Thirdly, I recommend that you look around the room.

This has its theory base from prehistoric times when the cave dwellers were confronted by a threat, i.e. a sabre-toothed tiger. Was it going to eat them? Were the cave dwellers going to eat it? Do I sprint away?

By calmly looking around the room you are about to speak in, we are saying to our prehistoric brain that there is no threat and there is no need to run. This allows the prefrontal cortex to think rationally. So just think that this speaking is an opportunity to show people what you know rather than see it as a threat.

Again, to counteract potential nerves and give clarity of performance, as was the case with Michael Phelps and Anthony Watson, we can use a series of visualisation techniques. These could be around specific mechanical and environmental scenarios or could be a complete distraction like visualising a beach scene or being high on a mountain top (See Lesson 10).

Another more distracting technique is to imagine the audience is naked and they are vulnerable, not you!

When speaking at national educational conferences, I used to find the smaller, close-up audiences much more intimidating, in the early days at least. To win over the audience, and calm my nerves, I now start to engage with the whole process. I began with what I call a distractor, e.g. asking for a round of applause for staff or sponsors. This allows me to test out the microphone and take a few breaths. I then look for something amusing to say such as a line from Don Black (2020):

"May I thank some dedicated people for making today possible for many people… the cardiologists, urologists and oncologists!"

Once I have the introductions out of the way, I might start to look for an ad-lib moment just to demonstrate that I am not a robot. Hopefully after a few laughs together, and not at my expense, the stage is set.

In my work I have also, from time to time, employed 'other techniques' to calm nerves and enhance performance.

This is what most professionals call their 'change toolkit'. Over the years, and even now, as I continually introduce new techniques, I am always curious to see what aligns with my ethos and what also may work for the people in front of me.

Examples of these include hypnotherapy, neuro-linguistic programming, integral eye-movement therapy, and emotional freedom technique.

In the past I might have dismissed these out of hand, but these days I open to leaning into 'stuff' that might help someone, hence my continued CPD in these areas. But I have a caveat. My ethos and philosophy is built upon my belief that creating positive change may indeed take a combined approach which almost always has its basis in some supporting work beyond a potential quick fix.

An example of my approach to change is based upon four principles:

1. Rapport and connection with the person. This will usually involve a shared empathy, respect and a belief I can help. This can be achieved online, but is so much more effective face to face.
2. The person must really want to explore the real possibility of sustained change and not just be looking for a quick fix – I call this 'convenience change'.
3. Both parties must be open to exploring different ways to create positive change – this is often a process that is often more about ruling techniques out than in.
4. The person must put in the hard yards with their planning, practising, reviewing and polishing their performance.

Finally, if you want my take on enjoying performance, try to engage yourself in the whole process, specifically look to engage with the audience. Use stories that show problems and reveal the solutions slowly to make the audience curious. Rather than see the experience as a threat, look forward to the event and see it as an opportunity to share your knowledge and expertise. Think of all the hard work you have done to get there, maybe years of effort and study.

If you are speaking, you are the expert in the room and people have come to listen to you. If you are about to sit an exam, you should be excited that you are getting the opportunity to share your knowledge, especially if you have put in countless hours of studying and revising.

A Tip From Alan Shearer

At the 2024 Euros when England performed perfectly in the quarter-final penalty shoot-out, Alan Shearer was quoted as saying, "Pressure is for tyres". This approach is basically about not even thinking about pressure as it 'doesn't apply to me'. Again, this is just one approach – in Lesson 10 we introduce staying with the pressure using ACT.

Even the most famous of speakers can get it wrong. Notable in this are politicians who should be used to speaking under the gaze of the media and its incumbent pressures. In the past year or so, Boris Johnson, former UK Prime Minister, and former US President Joe Biden, have made spectacular mistakes. Maybe it was these very public speaking mistakes that led to their downfall?

Deep Dive – Connectivity & Collaboration – Brené is Not Browned Off

In performance or daily communications, we often need to connect with our audience, be that one person or several thousand. Connectivity is a key human emotion and a skill that, once mastered, can open many doors. Some people go as far as to say that when we connect anything is possible.

Dr Brené Brown is an American professor who has written countless articles and books on being connected, being brave in life and vulnerability. She backs up her ideas with documented evidence including various longitudinal surveys – she is a professional who needs to be heeded. She often recounts a story of connectivity when she went to watch Sydney play Liverpool in a soccer match in Australia with two sets of fans, each wanting their team to win.

Before the match, the famous Liverpool anthem of 'You'll Never Walk Alone' was played. At that one moment, the whole crowd of 93,000 fans from both teams rose to their feet simultaneously to sing. She described a sensation where the hairs on the back of her neck started to tingle and she felt connected as one team, not two. This was the power of connectivity, and it binds human beings together for a common cause (Brené Brown, 2017).

There are studies into this connectivity when people sing in a choir. Not only is it empowering being all together with a common cause, but there is some evidence to suggest that chronic pain can be reduced when singing. This choral connection comes about through the power of collaboration.

I witnessed this recently when I attended a Summer fête in Saddleworth, and a SEN choir was singing to the crowd. I could not believe or fully comprehend the joy and extreme happiness that was exuding from each and every singer. Belonging to a choir and singing to an audience amplified their spirits. It made them feel worthy, accepted and happy. The crowd returned this feeling, and everyone was blissfully connected.

Nessun Need to Worry Russell

Another powerful example of connection and collaboration came when I was working as pitch-side host at PNEFC. The date was December 28th, 1999 and Preston were at home to Welsh team Wrexham. It was a damp, cloudy day, and the goalless football was not cheering anybody up.

At half-time, I had the privilege of introducing an unknown opera singer, on his debut performance in a sports stadium. He was going to sing 'Nessun Dorma' to win over an uninspiring crowd. After a few moments of singing, the crowd of some thirteen thousand started to boo him.

Unaccustomed to this style of music, and with no connection to either side, the torrent of abuse continued. But, as the unknown soloist built towards the chorus, the derision started to subside. Something special was happening. Launching into the chorus, he started to sing in his most powerful range. Most of the Wrexham fans stood up and started to applaud him.

This was swiftly followed by the home support. In a matter of seconds, the entire stadium was applauding, almost drowning out the song. To me, this was the moment this opera singer took a huge leap forward in his career. His name was Russell Watson.

Other forms of collaboration will occur in the workplace and are viewed as a positive step in the right direction. Collaboration requires you to facilitate others, respect their viewpoints and come to a joint conclusion – all actions of a high-level professional team. This is collectively termed Facilitation, and we will elaborate on this in Lesson 11.

To do this effectively you might have to be vulnerable. *What does this mean?*

Deep Dive – Vulnerability – Surgeons – Do You Trust Them?

To answer this, it might mean asking others for advice, or simply saying, 'I don't know'. On a more complex level, it could mean being brave and sharing your innermost vulnerabilities. When we show some vulnerability, it often brings others closer to you and can help you achieve your goals.

An example of this might be two equally qualified and experienced surgeons. One, who is keen to show that he knows everything, provides generically comprehensive and plausible answers, even if he is not absolutely certain of every possible outcome of a course of treatment.

The second surgeon answers equally comprehensively, but when asked about specific possible side effects on patients, he says he does not know, but will find out, thus showing some 'nice vulnerability'. I believe this draws people in closer to you.

(?) *Which surgeon would you trust more?*

Being connected, collaborating together and being vulnerable, do fit together naturally. As we age, it becomes more evident. We can be less competitive, but with the benefit of being more connected, collaborative and vulnerable. If you want better performance, this is the way to go. Focus less on knowledge transfer and focus more on a gentle, understanding approach to learning and learners.

(?) *Have you altered your approach to communicating with others over the years?*

A final point. Try and engage with feedback post-performance. You do not have to agree with it, but you might pick up some smart pointers. Even engaging in the feedback process is positive and can bring people on side.

Anti-Heroes

There are a small breed of performers who seem neither to be worried or interested in the audience and their emotions. They do not need approval or confirmation. These people are almost laws unto themselves, and you may fall into this category which I call anti-heroes.

They are like the footballer Mario Balotelli, Johnny Rotten of the Sex Pistols, or some comedians who thrive on insulting the crowd. I suspect deep down there may be a hidden need to be accepted, and perhaps, this outwardly condescending performance is their calling card and their way of dealing with the spotlight?

Lawro Doesn't Care

The former footballer and TV pundit Mark Lawrenson perhaps falls into this category. Having interviewed 'Lawro' several times, it became clear very quickly that he is not a nervous person. Indeed, he is the epitome of confidence, but with a wry edge.

He always kept me on my toes if I strayed with a question, or misquoted something. He would pounce with his dry humour and turn the spotlight on me, and in so doing, often got the audience on his side, which was a very smart move.

Lawro doesn't need the accreditation of the audience, he knows who he is, and you either like him or you don't. For the record, I believe most people not only like him, but respect him for his forthright and articulate views.

An Academic Heavyweight Knows How to Get Attention & Connect

Not really an anti-hero, maybe more of an old, seasoned maverick, was someone I only met once, who could only be described as a British academic heavyweight, and he had his own ways of connecting with the audience.

I did not fully know his pedigree before I met him when we were both speakers at a Heads annual conference in 2019. As I read his biography in the programme notes before he spoke, it was impressive. Former Oxbridge graduate who became a teacher, a high-level educationalist with a prominent county council, a professor of education, and a chief education officer at two education authorities.

Now in his late seventies, he dressed down for the occasion, rejecting protocol. He would dress in whatever was comfortable, and say what he liked, as I was about to find out. When he started speaking, something was different about his manner.

For an older man, he had the swagger of a much younger person. He started off by immediately launching into a story about a chance meeting with a fellow county education officer who he had bumped into on the high street in Birmingham. The anecdote went something like this:

"How are you doing? I know so much about you and your educational background, you're almost like a hero to me. What are you doing in Birmingham?"

The erudite academic's response was very direct, and left the person with no ambiguity about how he felt about being approached.

"Piss off!"

The whole place went deathly quiet. The audience and I were clearly not expecting this from a person of such very high standing.

He quickly explained that he loved to work as his mantra was 'the more I work the more I live, but sometimes people just got up my nose'. But he stressed that he was very glad to be working formally today. The audience fell about laughing in relief.

He broke the ice in his peerless way and connected with the audience instantly. He held them in the palm of his hand for the remaining forty-five minutes. At the end of his talk, he finished with a gem that was not only funny, but it linked back to the start of his presentation:

"In life, it is difficult to hate someone, like that annoying educational professional who accosted me out of nowhere on the streets of Birmingham... but in his case, it was well worth the effort!"

Famous Example of Connectivity – Lucy Meacock Starts Before it Starts

During the pandemic I was interviewed several times on Granada TV with a view to sharing my mental health expertise. On one occasion, before we went live on air, experienced TV presenter Lucy Meacock asked me several mental health questions on a couch in a quiet corner away from the TV studio. She also engaged in friendly chit-chat about other things in life.

I later realised that this was the way she got people to relax, by having a brief one-to-one, to connect first off-air. This pre-discussion builds connection and also helps any nerves disappear. That is exactly what happened when we went live.

She is a clever connected professional and believes in the idiom:

"*It starts before it starts.*" (Ross McWilliam, YouTube, *Granada Reports*)

"*To live with courage, purpose, and connection, to be the person whom we long to be, we must again be vulnerable. We must show up and let ourselves be seen.*" Dr Brené Brown (1965–present) American professor, author, researcher, storyteller, Tedx speaker and podcast host who has contributed extensively to academic literature.

SONOMA Waypoint Wisdom 50:

The opportunity to perform can happen in a heartbeat, and the impact can last a lifetime. Sometimes in life, especially in the Autumn of our lives, there is only a one-time opportunity to perform, so forget the nerves, be brave and grab the opportunity with both hands before somebody else does.

SONOMA Waypoint Wisdom 51:

When somebody *bee-lieves* in you, it can make you feel you really do have talent. Indeed, it gives you a *buzz* to reach your potential.

SONOMA Waypoint Wisdom 52:

Visualisation and performance go together. If you want more consistent performances, try and use both positive visualisation and negative troubleshooting visualisation. Preparing for all eventualities means you're preparing for success.

SONOMA Waypoint Wisdom 53:

The use of aspirations, confirmations and even humour can relax a performer. The secret is to find out which works best for you.

SONOMA Waypoint Wisdom 54:

At the end of the day, people will probably remember you more for how you made them feel, rather than what they learnt.

SONOMA Waypoint Wisdom 55:

High-level performance may have an element of nervous tension, i.e. being optimally adrenalised. But to excel, you must know your subject and, crucially, you must form a connection and develop curiosity with your audience. When this is in place, enjoyment is possible.

SONOMA Waypoint Wisdom 56:

Being vulnerable can be a key strength rather than a weakness. But be careful with whom you are vulnerable. Once you find the courage to be vulnerable it binds people to you. Link this to the power and human need of being connected, and the benefits of collaboration, then your progress is inevitable.

SONOMA Waypoint Wisdom 57:

Feedback is effective when it's immediate, accurate and specific. It can come from line manager, a test, delegates, independent observers or peers. Peer feedback is often the most accurate.

SONOMA Waypoint Wisdom 58:

When we are gentle and approachable, with less obsession on knowledge transfer, people can naturally gravitate to you. We can then tell our story with passion which connects the audience to give profound results.

QR Code Express Conversations & Mind Exercises into...
Seeing & Anchoring the Future

Measure your performance and add scores to the PSCP Matrix at the end of the book

Personal Sonoma Colour Profile –
7: Measurement of Performance Components

An accurate measure of performance would cover aspects of confidence, belief in one's abilities, ability to handle pressure, ability to practise and be resilient to challenges, and ability to connect, collaborate and be vulnerable with others.

Answer Always, Sometimes, or Never

1. I believe in myself even when things don't quite go the way I want.

2. I can adapt to challenges mid-performance.

3. I am willing to deliver a performance at short notice.

4. I like to thoroughly prepare for a performance.

5. I seek feedback after my performances.

6. I try to engage with the audience.

7. I am prepared to deliver a presentation but am willing to ad-lib if necessary.

8. If I become nervous, I have ways of using this positively.

9. I can open up to people and be vulnerable about my strengths and weaknesses.

Scoring
Always = 3, Sometimes = 2, Never = 1

Sonoma Gold = 19-27
You are a consummate professional and thrive on the opportunity to speak in public. Not only can you adapt to change, or even problems, but you can actually thrive on this disruption. A great blend of performance and ad-lib skills make you a standout performer.

Sonoma Silver = 10-18
You can perform and have had some success in the past. There is room for improvement, whether that is controlling nerves better, going more spontaneous in certain situations or simply employing more practice and belief.

Sonoma Bronze = 1-9
There may be an element of nervousness and reticence to your public speaking, but you can still pull it off. Once you commit to this process you can perform to a good level. Probably need more support, feedback and enhanced motivation.

Lesson 8:

Expected Wilters & Evergreen Climbers

Selective Procrastination, Versatility, Clarity, Patience, Less Intensity, Altruism & Philanthropy

Hidden Story – Tom & Jerry are Like Cat & Mouse

Tom and Jerry, a married middle-aged couple, were having a discussion. Tom was saying that the more he does, the less he seems to achieve and the more frustrated he becomes. Once one thing is done, something else needs doing; demands from his children, his work colleagues and even his friends at the golf club. He is running around in circles just to please everyone else. He does not want to let anyone down, but he wonders for how long he can sustain this. Jerry asked him to be more specific and cite an example:

"Well, I clear all my emails every day, but it seems even more appear the next day. Yesterday, I received a booking, and I immediately processed the request which took me ten minutes. Lo and behold, the customer emails back to cancel."

Jerry nods empathetically.

Tom feels he is burning himself out and is experiencing a range of unsavoury emotions such as dejection, anger and apathy. He often thinks to himself, *if this is what life is like now, what do I have to look forward to in retirement?*

Jerry has a different view at her time of life. Like her husband she enjoys her job, and she likes to support people inside and outside of work, and she will often volunteer to take some of the jobs off Tom. However, a key difference between them is that Jerry does not feel the need to do things straight away.

Rather, she prefers to employ selective procrastination, i.e. waiting or delaying an action. By doing so, a problem that is not urgent may actually resolve itself, or even just thinking about a challenge can give her a different outlook and maybe prompt her to approach it in a different, more effective way.

Sometimes she has no choice but to act immediately, but the more she employs strategic procrastination, the less frustrated she becomes and the more time she saves. Tom interrupts Jerry:

"Okay then, Jerry, give me an example of this great selective procrastination?"

"Simple. Last week, Fred from the golf club rang up asking if I could help him with the club accounts. I said I would look at them sometime that week. As it got to the end of the week, I still had not carved out enough time to get to the golf club. So, being polite, I called Fred to tell him not to worry, but I would pop round first thing Monday next week. When I spoke to Fred on Monday, I received a nice surprise. Fred had decided that he had better have a go at the accounts as it was about time he started to be a little more independent as he felt guilty asking me all the time."

Tom nodded in amazement. Jerry gave Tom another example:

"I often travel to London via train to do some consulting work for an international company. However, sometimes when they give me a work date and I book the tickets straight away, they can change my work date. So now when they give me a work date, I wait a few days, then call them back to confirm if it's still going ahead. Only then do I book the tickets."

As a result of this approach, Jerry has a little more time, is a little more relaxed, and is looking forward to whatever life throws at her. This selective procrastination often solves challenges without actually doing anything.

As the years pass, Tom is still stuck in his immediate 'job ticking off' list and 'people-pleasing' routine. He has backed himself into a cul-de-sac of behaviours. As a coping mechanism he has started to smoke and drink more. Sometimes he stops out late or he goes to bed early – both avoidance behaviours. He is constantly working and operating at one hundred per cent with no extra capacity. His physical health has started to wane, and he has developed some mental health challenges. He feels more worn out every day. He is heading to burn-out, or worse.

Jerry rarely works at one hundred per cent, preferring to work at about eighty per cent so she can have something in the tank if she needs to help out in an emergency. Even though she works at this active capacity, she is still perceived as a team player and is equally respected by her family, work colleagues and the wider community.

Tom's grumpy, erratic and avoidant behaviour has an impact on the couple. They drift apart. Without the close support of his wife, Tom spirals downwards. He lives out a lonely, unfulfilled life dogged by ill health and dies long before he should have done.

Jerry is shocked and saddened, but her life must go on. In many ways, both lose out: Jerry lost her husband, and Tom lost his life. The irony is, that this could have turned out so differently if selective strategic procrastination had been observed. This is a lesson to us all – if we keep trying to tick off jobs immediately, being a people pleaser or just fulfilling an outmoded expectation of our role in life, soon there might not be a life.

Challenge

Be careful that selective procrastination is not interpreted as disrespectful. Some people in business and life expect, or even demand, immediate responses to requests. Know who the key players are within your business and communicate your terms of engagement to them.

As a rule of thumb, some organisations I have worked within have a rule of replying to an email within twenty-four hours, depending on the client. This is known as a service level agreement (SLA) or key performance indicator (KPI) that some measure themselves by both internally and/or externally. SLA's, for example, may be advertised as such for any given request or service applied for or have it simply as an automatic response email, i.e. *Thank you for your email, we will provide a response in the next… X… hours.*

Global Story – The Colonel is Home & Fried

Harland Sanders might not be an instantly recognised name. But his is a story of immense global success that involved a high degree of versatility. He had a number of jobs in his early life, such as steam engine stoker, firefighter, railway labourer, manager of a filling station and insurance salesperson. He also became a lawyer, but this ended when his reputation was destroyed after a fist fight with his own client. Yet this stubbornness and other instances of challenging authority was to be his strength.

He also had a passion for food and in his own time, he was developing a 'secret recipe' and a special pressure fryer method to cook his food that elicited a unique taste and was quicker than using a frying pan. He soon started to sell his favourite dish of fried chicken from a roadside restaurant with so much success that the Governor of Kentucky bestowed the highest honourary title of Colonel on him in 1935. Eventually, in 1952, aged sixty-two, he opened the first official franchise restaurant in South Salt Lake City, Utah. When this restaurant closed, he devoted his full attention to franchising his fried chicken brand across America.

In 1964, aged seventy-three, he sold the company for two million dollars which would now be worth over eighteen million dollars! The franchise brand was Kentucky Fried Chicken and the name which is synonymous with that brand was Colonel Sanders!

Harland 'Colonel' Sanders was very versatile, working in numerous jobs that did not suit his personality until later in life he discovered his passion. As a late business bloomer, he worked tirelessly to perfect his recipe and an air fryer method that could produce a consistent high-quality taste. The key common denominator seems to be a continual pursuit of a final product that could be consistently replicated, but not copied, as it was, and still is, a secret. (Wikipedia, Harland Sanders).

(?) *How many people become successful aged seventy-three?*

Taisto Carries His Wife Everywhere

Another global story of someone who has demonstrated supreme versatility, consistency and superhuman strength and stamina is the lesser-known Finnish world champion, Taisto Miettinen.

Born in 1965, his achievements so far, are gold medals for:

- World Champion Water Running (2004).
- Iron Bar Walking Champion (2012).
- Bog Snorkelling Champion (2012).
- Kicksled Champion (2014).
- Finnish Snowshoe Champion (2010, 2011, 2012, 2014).
- Finnish Winter Swimming Champion (2010).
- Wife Carrying World Champion (2009–2013, 2017, 2022) and he is the oldest contestant (aged fifty-seven) to win the World Championship in Wife Carrying.
- Ten World Championship Titles, Nineteen World Champion Medals, Eleven Finnish Championship Titles and Seventeen Foreign Countries Championship Medals.

Taisto Miettinen has been voted the World's Greatest Reigning Stupendous Unknown Champion Number One by CraveOnline. He is a lawyer, wrote a book on corporate tax, has entered politics and is a national and international guest on various TV shows (Wikipedia, Taisto Miettinen).

It just goes to show that as much as money and fame can be very alluring for some, for others, the attraction is the quest to be the best and consistently maintain it.

> *Maybe you don't aspire to be the best wife carrier in the world, but what do you do that doesn't involve money or fame, that you want to become the best at, or at least better at?*

My Story – 'When The Saints Go Marching In'

In 1993, I was accepted to study for a post-graduate certificate in education (PGCE) at the University of Southampton. I wanted to become a teacher of physical education. This was truly vocational, and it was a clear outcome, yet I had always thrived on variety and being versatile. A real contradiction for me. I need not have worried, as the skills and expertise I was going to acquire would make me both vocational and versatile to both employers, and self-employment.

With the new Dearing Review on Education (1994), there was a proliferation of many educational assessment and accountability changes that were being implemented nationwide and any course would have to embody these directives. We were going to represent a new breed of teachers who were not only up to speed with this new educational legislation but could offer versatile expertise that would fit most curricula. I also chose this course because the lecturers had a variety of ages, mixed genders, and contrasting areas of expertise. Given I was thirty-three years of age and ripe for development, it was an ideal place to become qualified. I was not disappointed.

Over the course of the next year, I was submerged into the latest education pedagogy, learnt about new assessment levels, how to be accountable in teaching and, crucially, became proficient in numerous sports, activities and even other academic subjects. The whole idea was to give you specificity of knowledge but within an applied versatile framework.

We were passing exams and being accredited in sports and activities such as gymnastics, badminton, football, rugby, health-related fitness, game dynamics, sailing, archery, outdoor activities, orienteering, etc. We were learning in situ in primary, secondary, tertiary and SEN school settings. Most weekends our versatility was tested as we could be sailing down the Solent, orienteering in the Brecon Beacons or mountain biking in the New Forest.

Alternatively, we would be learning a second subject, so that we would ultimately become irresistible to prospective employers. This versatile approach to learning matched the new educational changes and every single person who applied for a teaching job from our graduate intake in September 1994 comfortably managed to secure employment.

As our careers subsequently developed, and our bodies started to deteriorate, many of us demonstrated our versatility by teaching our second subjects, mine being information communication technology (ICT). I eventually became Head of ICT in a small Emotional Behavioural School.

The versatile training I had been given at Southampton, and the school placements, has stood me in good stead. Coupled with my employment at PNEFC, these experiences have allowed me to successfully transition into speaking, training and writing. With this richness, diversity and versatility of training and experiences, I have been able to reinvent myself. Sadly, though, without the financial remuneration of the Colonel, or the strength of Taisto, but with the satisfaction of helping people.

Deep Dive – Professional Clarity – Pure Professionals

As we have already established, having versatility in our approach to our professional lives can have rewarding outcomes, but this might take time. Yet, ironically, if we want success more immediately, we may have to be more direct and opt for a vocational approach. I call this 'professional clarity'.

There are certain professions where there are clear professional pathways that must be traversed and mastered, i.e. doctors, vets, solicitors, accountants, pilots, pathologists, etc. You are taught a clear discipline of skills often over an extended period of time. Being vocationally inclined at an early age can reap benefits in mid-life, that will almost definitely last a lifetime, often with very few risks attached. These professions will always exist, so job security is high and is often matched by high remuneration for low risk. That is a very good return on investment (ROI).

Deep Dive – Versatility Switch Hitters

But what about a blended approach, of using a vocational platform initially, that develops into a versatile, multi discipline career later in life?

Examples of this could be:

- **Clint Eastwood** – Actor, Director, Mayor, Activist.
- **Jeff Bezos** – Entrepreneur, Media Proprietor, Astronaut.
- **Elon Musk** – Business Magnate, Investor, Space X Owner.
- **Vera Wang** – Figure Skater, Journalist, Fashion Designer.
- **Steven Bartlett** – Entrepreneur Social Media Marketing.

For many people, this initial clear vocational approach is often like getting to first base. Once achieved and a platform secured, other opportunities either start to open up, or are actively pursued.

This may be a mistake many younger prospective high-flying professionals make – they diversify too soon. I do believe in being vocational, at least initially, developing your knowledge and craft, and then switch hit.

Deep Dive – Philanthropy & Altruism

Beyond this first and second base success, others might develop into serial philanthropists, which is where someone donates their money, time, talent or skills to help others and create a better world. Technically, this is called altruism – or we could call it making a home run from second or third base. These people have a business platform from which they can positively influence others for no self-gain. Examples of this could be:

- **Bill Gates** – Former Microsoft Co-Founder and Gates Foundation.
- **Warren Buffet** – Business Investor Berkshire Hathaway and The Giving Pledge Co-Creator.
- **Paul Tudor Jones** – Tudor Hedge Fund Manager and Robin Hood Foundation.
- **Andrew Carnegie** – Steel industry Magnate and Carnegie Charity Custodian.
- **Diane Von Fürstenberg** – Designer and Diller Von Fürstenberg Family Foundation.
- **MacKenzie Scott** – Acclaimed Novelist and Giving Pledge.

As we shall see in Lesson 10, helping others can actually improve your health span and increase your life span. Maybe these people are onto something?

What else can we learn from these highly successful individuals?

Deep Dive – Patience – You Might Have to Wait for Success

How many people today want and adopt a fast track to success strategy? How many of these people achieve this in five years, ten years, or ever?

From all the examples above, one quality or attribute is

clearly evident – patience. This can be a collective structured organisational mindset, or an individual patience, where responses are less immediate and haphazard, and more structured and coordinated.

Not one of either the philanthropists, the blended success professionals or even the Colonel himself, got success overnight, and some are still trying. Many are older, wiser and maybe richer for their journeys.

Deep Dive – Less Intensity – With Balance, Authenticity, Empathy & Kindness

But there is something else which I feel makes some people successful. That quality is hard to define, but comes from a place that has *balance, authenticity, empathy, and kindness* – a less intense, and more relaxed approach to business and life. It seems to be less of a hard push approach and more of a soft pull approach, getting people on board, rallying the collective herd, seeing the overall picture and coordinating resources for the benefit of others.

This less serious and more relaxed approach from time to time can get you a long way. In competitive business, it is sadly lacking, and is almost seen as a weakness.

As I have aged, I have tried to adopt this less intense approach more: being authentically interested in others, being gentle, understanding and preparing for specific needs, being patient for outcomes and seeing the bigger picture.

When I am working with high-flying professionals in the corporate world or senior leadership school teams, I often try and put people at ease first instead of hitting them with harsh knowledge transfer. A friendly smile, inviting questions, and asking for their agenda, are all part of my softer and more relaxed approach. By doing this you give out the aura of calmness and authenticity.

Too often, I have seen and worked with, super-efficient, busy professionals who might get the job done, but make everyone around them feel tense, and subsequently more likely to underperform. More often than not, they make me feel nervous.

A case in point is a party host, who is super-efficient, but could not stop, even for a chat with VIP guests who were making polite conversation and asking questions. The event may have gone well, but there was a feeling of panic that transmitted via the host to everyone.

Try and laugh when you could cry, or respond with simple acceptance if things have not gone that well. Be calm but also relaxed, not taking everything to heart or too literally – get some perspective. See the bigger picture, have that reflective 'helicopter view', then return to the scene in a better place professionally and emotionally.

Your responses will ultimately define you. You might be hyper-demanding, angry or even aggressive occasionally, and get a great response. But if you do it all the time, you wear people out. They can begin to resent you, or they simply avoid or ignore you. Indeed, a leader with a far too intense approach can amplify tension within the environment in a brutal and destructive fashion.

Which leaders have you worked for that engender tension with unremitting demands on your time, energy and acumen. Has this ended in bitter acrimony, or even dismissal of either the boss or yourself?

One final point about kindness. This quality can have somewhat of a virtue signalling dimension, i.e. some people pretend to be kind, and yet their actions leave much to be desired. You will know a kind person when their kind words align with their kind actions. I encountered an example of this kindness in 1994 when I was teaching in Southampton.

I was on teaching practice at Weston Secondary, and as a PE teacher, there were always plenty of after-school clubs and activities to help out with. After one particularly busy week, following several weeks of establishing my worth and eagerness to learn and help out, I finished around 5.30pm.

As I was wearily leaving school, PE bags in hand, and a long forty-minute walk ahead of me back to my digs, I heard the Head teacher call out:

"Would you like a lift home?"

"Thank you, but it's out of your way," I replied, knowing that this particular Head lived in an area of Southampton that was far away from the student area I would be returning to.

"It might be out of my way, but that's okay. You would do the same for me if the roles were reversed?" he replied.

I nodded and accepted the lift, richer for the extra lesson in kindness.

I know why I haven't forgotten about this incident almost thirty years later – it was an authentic kind gesture.

When was the last time you demonstrated a truly altruistic kind gesture, wanting nothing in return?

When we are constantly evolving, opportunities for development, progress and success will always be available, even more so when we show kindness.

Famous Example – A Football Master is Versatile & can Procrastinate

In 2001, I went to a training facility in north-west England to meet with a then giant of the football world for a prearranged visit. The reason I was there was to video him for a two-minute speech which we would use at a special celebratory dinner for legendary ex-Preston and England footballer, Sir Tom Finney.

This manager had a reputation that went before him for not suffering fools. A cameraman and I had agreed to meet and film at 9am before the players turned up. Slowly the clock ticked around to 10am and still there was no sign of him. Midday came and went, and we were getting frustrated. Questions popped into my head such as:

Is he ever going to show up? Who does he think he is anyway?

At 12.45pm he breezed into the room. He issued a very, very brief explanation for his lateness rather than an apology:

"Bloody players arguing… I had to sort it out myself! Then I had an agent wanting something or other, then the media wanted a piece of me. Right, we are here now, what do you want me to do… we have five minutes!"

"Can you deliver a two-minute speech about Sir Tom talking about his impact on you and his contribution to the game?" I said politely, despite my frustration at losing a morning's work.

He nodded. We set up the camera and microphone and then pointed it at him. Without hesitation, he started to espouse a story about Sir Tom, before talking about how Sir Tom's career had impacted players across the world. He finished the cameo to camera in one minute and fifty-nine seconds and it was word perfect with no hesitations or mistakes. It was then that it struck me how versatile he was dealing with a variety of football matters in such a short space of time.

He had viewed our meeting as something he could procrastinate on, so he could deal with these more pressing matters. Then he did something that further surprised me. Probably as a nod to the way we had waited patiently, he motioned across to two high-profile players to sign some shirts and say a few words for the video recording. This was probably his way of saying sorry as he recognised his own lateness and our patience.

In his day, he was a very intense manager who used strict discipline to achieve his goals. His management style was at times very confrontational and when anyone got out of line he would be very direct. However, I believe a large part of this was because he cared about the players and wanted them all to reach their potential.

He had a nurturing side that was often overlooked. Many ex-players have said this and having met him, I felt that this was a quality that was often misunderstood as people wanted to paint him first and foremost as a disciplinarian.

"*Life isn't about finding yourself. Life is about creating yourself.*" George Bernard Shaw (1856–1950) Irish playwright, critic, and political activist.

SONOMA *Waypoint Wisdom* 59:

Work out when getting things ticked off your list is serving you and when it is hurting you.

SONOMA *Waypoint Wisdom* 60:

Selective procrastination can work for us, but not 24/7. Knowing when to respond and when to delay is strategic selective procrastination.

SONOMA *Waypoint Wisdom* 61:

Being versatile may mean being able to adapt to lifestyle and career changes, withstanding and benefiting from disappointments and producing a final product that can be consistently replicated but is difficult to copy.

SONOMA *Waypoint Wisdom* 62:

You may get lucky and steal a home run in your get rich quick approach to business. It is very high risk, and you may spend a lifetime chasing it. Rather, decide on professional clarity or a blended approach, and stick to it. The rewards for yourself and others could be astronomical and altruistic.

SONOMA *Waypoint Wisdom* 63:

Learning from the journey over time may be the only sure way to reach your destination. Develop patience on this journey and do not be in a rush to arrive!

SONOMA Waypoint Wisdom 64:

To engage either with an audience or an individual, try and understand their needs. By showing an authentic interest in others, you will endear them which will make knowledge transfer or discussions more effective.

SONOMA Waypoint Wisdom 65:

Adopt a less intense approach that involves balance, authenticity, empathy and kindness. Create that pull towards you rather than a constant push and demand on people.

SONOMA Waypoint Wisdom 66:

Without a varied approach in business and life, we will end up becoming less effective, with people starting to resent us.

QR Code Express Conversations & Mind Exercises into...
Clarity & Less Intensity

Measure your performance and add scores to the PSCP Matrix at the end of the book

Personal Sonoma Colour Profile –
8: Measurement of Qualities & Skills

Selective procrastination, versatility, clarity, patience and less intensity are difficult to measure, either individually, or collectively. Nevertheless, try these questions:

Answer Always, Sometimes or Never

1. Do you have patience for your life?

2. Do you have a clear vision for your life?

3. Have you the ability to reactively reinvent yourself?

4. Can you reinvent yourself proactively?

5. Can you employ strategic procrastination that creates a win-win for both you and the other party?

6. Can you employ a more relaxed, less intense approach with kindness, authenticity and empathy?

7. Can you envisage other ways of achieving success that may benefit you and others in the future?

8. Can you get things in perspective and see the bigger picture?

9. Can you demonstrate a balanced approach to work and life?

Scoring
Always = 3, Sometimes = 2, Never = 1

Sonoma Gold = 19-27
You are a very versatile and accomplished professional. You can see details, but also zoom out to see the bigger picture. You can maximise life and work opportunities to create that win-win scenario.

Sonoma Silver = 10-18
You are performing well to date but need to keep upskilling and reviewing your approach to work and life. With a more adaptive and creative approach, more success will be waiting for you.

Sonoma Bronze = 1-9
You can perform and win over people, but it doesn't always go right and it's becoming more difficult to develop. You can get drawn into situations which can deplete you and your resources. Now is the time to upskill and adopt a slightly different approach.

Lesson 9:

Gathering in the Crops – Nature's Grand Finale

Loyalty, Stress, Rust-Out, Flow, Burn-Out & Humour

Hidden Story – Mini, Midi & Maxi Fly Away or Not

Three kites were getting ready to go out and play in the wind. The first kite, Mini, did not like it too windy. She preferred to dance with a soft breeze that was not too taxing. She was happy just as long as she could do a little safe flying.

The second kite, Midi, quite liked flying. He could adapt to changes in wind strength and preferred flying in a steady Flow, but with some challenging winds.

The third kite, Maxi, adored flying in the wind, and the stronger the wind, the better.

Each day they played out together, but each day when they returned home they were never all happy. Some days Mini was happy because she could play softly. On other days Midi was happy because he could get a ride on a thermal updraft, test himself, and enjoy the wind.

Occasionally Maxi was very happy when he could really challenge himself in extreme windy conditions.

This carried on for several years. Then one day things changed forever. There was a strong gale and Maxi could not wait to get outside. Unfortunately, the gale ripped Maxi and he plummeted to the ground with a deadly thud. Maxi's flying days were over.

After a few weeks of just Mini and Midi flying, things changed again. Mini had become bored and did not want to fly anymore. Mini retired but was bored again almost immediately. Midi, though, was not finished. He continued to thrive and enjoyed many windy days when he challenged himself within his limits. Midi went on to win many competitions and eventually got promoted to head judge in the national kite competition.

The moral of the story is beware how you set your kite out in life:

- Some people set out to achieve everything almost all at once and will do anything to achieve it. These people may achieve some success but there might be a price to pay, sometimes it is a very hefty price. These people are called Burn-Outs.
- Some people set out to achieve very little and prefer to go under the radar which is fine – it is their choice. However, without being challenged and opting for an easy life, they can soon become resistant to any new stress or change. These people are called Rust-Outs.
- Some people set out to achieve, but not at all costs. They see life as a series of challenges, and they use these challenges to develop themselves. They know when

they need more challenges, and they know when they are being over-challenged. These people are called Flow.

Global Story – Hachikō is Loyal to the End

I will wait for you, no matter how long it takes.

This is a tagline from a poster, and it refers to the quality of loyalty and unquestioning devotion displayed by Hachikō.

Hachikō was born in Japan in 1923 and abandoned at birth. He was adopted by Hidesaburō Ueno, a renowned professor of agriculture. Several times a week, Ueno would take a train and Hachikō would walk with him to the station. Hachikō would wait patiently and loyally at the train station until Ueno returned.

In 1925, Ueno unexpectedly passed away, but Hachikō was not informed. He was now alone. He was passed around to other families, but was not happy. Soon Hachikō was returning to the train station daily, waiting for Ueno to return, hopeful that one day he would be reunited.

When the evening train arrived, Hachikō would look at each passenger as if he were looking for Ueno. This carried on for several years and in 1932 a local Japanese newspaper wrote an article about him. Very quickly after the article was published, Hachikō received donations of food, poems were written about him, and he received visitors from far and wide.

With proceeds from a fund-raising event, a statue was erected of him in 1934. Sadly, in 1935 Hachikō died, and his death reached the front page of many national newspapers. At his funeral, Buddhist monks offered prayers for him, and dignitaries read eulogies. Thousands visited his statue in the following days. Following World War II, eight hundred thousand yen was raised for a new statue of Hachikō. Every year on April 8th a memorial service is held for Hachikō to remember the value of keeping faith and loyalty in someone.

Hachikō is the most famous dog in Japanese history (*BBC News*, 2023).

Challenge

Loyalty is a quality that seems to be in short supply in some aspects of modern society. It is also underrated, especially compared to society's expectations of yesteryear.

Equally, do not let loyalty be an excuse for someone to keep pressurising you into unreasonable demands based on prior loyalty expectations. This testing of loyalty is not acceptable and must be stood up to before it develops into a situation where one person needs to leave the organisation or jettison 'friends'. I have sadly witnessed this on more than one occasion. Remember, you don't have to stand up alone – enlist support.

Have you ever jettisoned friends, like James Altucher in Lesson 1? If so, why?

My Story – Derian Humour is One Way to Deal With a Difficult Situation

Over the years I have contributed to various charities such as Bladder Cancer Research (following my father's death), Dementia Care (following my mother's death), St Catherine's Hospice, Baby Beat at Royal Preston Hospital, and The British Heart Foundation. However, a charity that became very dear to me was Derian House Children's Hospice in Chorley. The then CEO, Georgina Cox, asked me and my fellow trainer, Colin Dixon, to deliver a couple of days' training and learning to several terminally ill young adults aged sixteen to nineteen.

In many ways, it was a difficult assignment. Firstly, would these children engage with us about motivation, self-esteem, aspiration, growth mindsets and resilience?

Secondly, many of the children were confined to wheelchairs, so how could we get involvement and engagement? Thirdly, many had sight and hearing difficulties, a side effect of very strong cancer drugs.

Finally, would the children have the stamina and desire to listen to us for a whole day, let alone two?

I needn't have worried. The feedback from both days was really positive from both children and support staff.

But more importantly, what did they teach me?

The very thing that struck me was their humour, sometimes it was very dark, but often it was their way of breaking the ice around a difficult subject like aspiration for the future:

"I am going to start saving for my pension!" and "I aspire to keep alive!"

Humour can deflect attention away from serious issues. I do not believe it demeans their challenges, but I think it was a welcome relief to laugh for all concerned. Humour also allows for a reset, a natural or contrived break, before learning starts again. People often say, "*if you don't laugh, then you will cry*" and I sensed this cliché was entirely accurate at Derian House. In fact, for some children, humour and laughter was their main coping strategy.

What else did I learn from the children at Derian House?

Given that every young person in the room would probably die within the year, I was very surprised that many had a passion for something in the form of a hobby or interest. This was something that they held onto dearly. Was this as a symbol of hope, or simply one of the few distractions to look forward to?

I was there over the two days to see if I could help them with their hobbies and interests and grow their passion more, with bits of knowledge and experiences. For example, one child asked me how they could develop their memory. I did not question why, but maybe it had something to do with examinations and proving to others that they could pass, that they were worth something. This passion to prove something abounded in that room and at the very heart of it I believe was self-esteem and the human need to be valued, cared for and loved.

Often when I have worked with very disadvantaged schoolchildren, in various institutions, two common missing ingredients are passion and humour. It is almost like their current adversity has overtaken them and they cannot see a way out. Who could blame them given what little I knew about their challenging backgrounds.

At Derian, life expectancy was very short, but it did not stop the children searching for recognition and using humour at every appropriate or inappropriate moment. I will never forget one darkly humourous comment as we reached the end of the first day:

"Give us whatever homework you want, Ross; chances are we won't be here to finish it when you return!"

I still remember those Derian sessions of 2013 and many of the faces who will no longer be with us. Not only do I remember, but I try and instil a sense of passion and humour into my professional and personal activities as a result of this experience.

Being serious and learning is a good thing but not 24/7, and certainly not when adversity is hanging heavily around your shoulders. As we have seen already, the ability to lighten situations, where appropriate, and be less intense, can be what defines and separates professionals. Often when hope is lost, there can seem little point in life and humour can then be used to mask over very serious situations. In a strange way, humour and hope go together.

Have you used humour in desperate times, and did it help the situation?

I have seen this use of diminished hope and humour only once before, when somebody I knew was very down, and maybe was clinically depressed. One day he seemed to change overnight and became very outgoing, using light and dark humour to appear as if a weight had been lifted from his shoulders. Sadly, a weight had been lifted, as he had decided to end his life on a specific date in the future, and now he was intent on enjoying his last few weeks. I learnt very quickly that this was a trait of some suicides.

Deep Dive – Stress – Our Friend as Well as Our Enemy?

As we have already seen with Mini, Midi and Maxi, our approach to life can have a major impact on our physical and emotional health. Often we use the word stress when we are fighting something, and it is wearing us out, i.e. it is a negative thing. However, the word stress, which was used extensively by Walter Gannon in the 1920s and Dr Hans Selye in the 1940s, was originally created to explain that humans need challenges or stresses for them to develop and grow. But, when the *frequency*, *intensity* and/or *duration* of the stress outweighs our ability to respond effectively, that is when stress becomes dangerous to us. This is often called the FID approach.

Indeed, researchers often quote stress as a good quality if it is in context with a person's ability to manage FID. Dr Alia Crum (2021) and Dr Kelly McGonigal (2015), Stamford University psychologists, talk about the benefits of stress. In particular, how it can help us beat a challenge, and how, if viewed positively, can make us healthier and maybe even live longer! In short, they argue that we should view stress as an enabler, and we should lean into it.

Stress is natural and we just need to learn how to embrace it rather than be afraid of it, says Crum. Often, we think we do not have the resources or skillset in a stressful situation, but we could be generalising our response to that stress. In fact, stress can enable us to perform better by giving us a challenge.

To beat stress we first must:

1. Accept and recognise that we are a little stressed – this is awareness and acceptance. Identify your behavioural and physiological changes.
2. Welcome your stress and even lean into it – it is your body getting ready to respond because you care about this situation and it probably reflects your purpose.
3. Use your feelings around purpose, to figure out and implement a positive response.

McGonigal has redefined what she thought about stress. Back in 2013, in a Ted Talk (that has since been downloaded over thirty million times), she came to the conclusion that stress was very harmful. Since then, she believes that not only is stress good for us, but it can also prolong life – it all depends on how you view stress. Just thinking that stress is harmful, can adversely affect life expectancy. Rather, believe that stress is helpful, and it can prolong life.

A final point from McGonigal. Oxytocin, the love or cuddle hormone, is produced when we involve ourselves in human interactions. So, if you want to feel better, get socialising.

Deep Dive – Burn-Out & Toxic Stress Load Syndrome

When we get out of synchronicity with FID and we cannot cope with the stress demands, then we may encounter adverse effects such as Burn-Out. According to the International Classification of Diseases (ICD-11), Burn-Out as an occupational phenomenon is defined as: *A syndrome conceptualised as resulting from chronic workplace stress that has not been successfully managed. It is characterised by three dimensions:*

- Feelings of energy depletion or exhaustion.
- Increased mental distance from one's job, or feelings of negativism or cynicism related to one's job.
- Reduced professional efficacy.

Often, Burn-Out is stealthy, we do not know it is occurring, and it can be masked by thoughts and feelings around self-worth, self- and societal expectations, gender bias, and our overall Frame of Reference.

Similar to this, is the condition known as Toxic Stress Load (TSL) which is a build-up of physical and psychological changes that result from a need to respond to challenges. It is the baggage, the scars, and the tensions collected through life. When your TSL becomes overwhelming, it triggers changes in your body that are so profound that they are equivalent to accelerated ageing. Burn-Out and TSL need to be proactively reduced or avoided.

A recent study by the Society of Occupational Medicine (2023) says health staff are increasingly facing emotional exhaustion. It recommends manageable workloads, well-being training and improved staff support. NHS figures for February 2023 show 24.6 per cent of absences were due to anxiety, stress, depression and other psychiatric illnesses.

We must be careful, that in our quest to grow and develop, we don't get too close to damaging our mental health. In simple terms, we need to be aware where the learning zone ends and where stress development starts.

Two final points about stress:

1. According to Canadian physician and health writer, Gabor Maté (2019), when we repress stress this can have a life-shortening impact upon us, especially within women. When we consistently put others ahead of our own emotional needs, probably as a result of socially determined roles, we can leave ourselves open to various autoimmune diseases such as lupus, rheumatoid arthritis and thyroid disease. Up to eighty per cent of these cases occur within women.

2. Being under heavy stress shortens life expectancy by 2.8 years. These results were based on a study in which researchers from the Finnish Institute for Health and Welfare (1987–2007) calculated the effects of multiple risk factors, including lifestyle-related ones, to the life expectancy of men and women.

Often quoted, but not referenced (maybe it is an urban myth), is the common statement that teachers, prison officers and police officers experience high levels of stress in their profession, with excessive production of adrenaline and cortisol which can have a negative impact on life expectancy once they retire. With over thirty years' service, this type of professional has an average life expectancy of another eight years, or so the insurance companies who work this out would say!

The kicker is we are all probably going to find ourselves more compromised in life the older we get due to our inevitable failing health, which is not a nice thought, but one we must be prepared for. I believe you have to be strong to get old.

Deep Dive – Stress Actions

If we can be aware of our stress levels, maybe behave proactively, as well as reactively, then we may be able to harness the benefits of stress to enhance our career and life. A really simple way to start this awareness is by adopting two steps:

1. Write down your stress signature, i.e. what is it you do, or do not do, or say or do not say, or think or do not think, when you are overly stressed, and communicate this with others.

2. Ask your staff or family members to disclose their stress signatures and understand what helps them and what hurts them when they are stressed.

Here are six additional things that I do regularly to channel stress. They help me get events and life in context:

- **Happiness Hour** – Do something every day, for an hour, that not only brings you joy, but acts as a complete distraction from work.
- **Mindful Minute** – Catch yourself in stress and change your mood in a minute.
- **Magic Moment** – Every day look for at least one thing that went well, that brought a smile to your face.
- **Reward More & Expect Less** – Often we must have one hundred per cent to earn a reward. Try rewarding yourself when it is not quite one hundred per cent and at the same time relax your expectations a little – both actions will serve you well in the long term.
- **Compartmentalise** – Whenever I get a challenge, I try not to catastrophise. If I do, then I catch myself and stop

that thinking. Once I have addressed a specific action, I sit back and let the challenge be compartmentalised, until further action is needed.

- **Take Action**… at least make a decision.

Flow – Dickie Knows Best

For me I don't recognise when I am in Flow until I am out of Flow.

What do I mean by this?

Let me give you an example: When I was collecting all my permissions for the anecdotal stories, I felt it was a heavy burden and I was stressing about the task – would people say no, how long would it take, would they be insulted?

This weighed over me for quite a while. But as soon as I started to communicate with people and started to engage with the whole process, I felt very positive. The feedback I was getting was super-positive and reaffirmed my belief about the book and myself.

For five days, including a weekend, I was almost obsessive as I contacted all my contributors to get their permissions to include them in my stories. Very quickly, people got back to me often with more than I expected. I would work hours on end, even during the Euro football matches, as the whole process had grabbed my attention.

It was only when I had finished each section of collating stories, that I noticed the time and the TV programmes I had missed. For me, this is my true Flow.

A friend of mine, Richard Bamford, talks about Flow in life and once gave me an excellent axiom about how to look at life and business:

"It's easier to push against an opening door, rather than a closing or closed door."

So, as I age and gather more knowledge and experience, I search for doors where I can put this acumen. In my sixties, I am avoiding doors that resist and am searching for doors that swing open more smoothly. But when you're younger, you might have to push many resisting doors to see what is and is not possible.

Famous Example of Flow – It's Unbelievable Jeff... Bezos Wants Harmony

We mentioned Jeff Bezos in the previous Lesson, and he has clear views on this balance between work, and life outside work. He does not like the phrase 'work-life balance' as this by its very nature, infers a gain in one but at the expense of the other. Rather, Bezos prefers the term 'work-life harmony', where one fuels the other, like a symbiotic relationship where life is in Flow.

Guess how you can tell if you have this harmony or Flow right?

Imagine walking around a corner, and you cannot see a person on the other side of the bend. As soon as you come around the corner, a colleague or friend comes into view. What is their first reaction? If it is positive, smiling, glad, etc, then you have the right harmony. If it is less communicative, avoiding or even angry, then you probably do not have harmony!

"It's part of the cure to wish to be cured." Seneca The Younger (4BC–65AD). Philosopher, statesman and dramatist of Ancient Rome.

SONOMA Waypoint Wisdom 67:

Burn-Out can be quite stealthy and you might not see it coming until it is too late. Try and see stress as a facilitator to greater success, but be careful it is not a win at all costs pursuit.

SONOMA Waypoint Wisdom 68:

Rust-Out might seem like an attractive option, being under the radar and doing the bare minimum. But be careful what you wish for, as you will not develop your capacity for greater success. Equally, you could begin to loathe Rust-Out, but cannot get back into the game again.

SONOMA Waypoint Wisdom 69:

Flow is where we need to be more. See a challenge as an opportunity to grow and develop, but be aware if the *frequency*, *intensity* and *duration* of the stress is eating away at you, and pushing you towards Burn-out – look for the smooth swinging doors.

SONOMA Waypoint Wisdom 70:

Loyalty is a much understated quality be it in professional or personal life. Try and develop it in various ways as there may come a time when you 'drop the ball' and need someone else's loyalty.

SONOMA Waypoint Wisdom 71:

Loyalty is often developed through clear and consistent communication about roles, expectations and feedback. Ensure you 'show up' and 'be present' consistently.

SONOMA Waypoint Wisdom 72:

Always look for ways to incorporate appropriate humour. Sometimes it is the only thing we have to give and can often define us in our moments of greatest need.

SONOMA Waypoint Wisdom 73:

Your staff and even friends will not thank you for being serious 24/7. Finding opportunities to share thoughts and humour can be a great way to break the ice and thaw heated tensions.

SONOMA Waypoint Wisdom 74:

Aim for the middle ground of resilience performance, where we can take on challenges and thrive in Flow, rather than just try to survive in Rust-Out, or worse still, crash in Burn-Out with possibly fatal consequences.

SONOMA Waypoint Wisdom 75:

Get to know your own stress signature and those of your staff or family and know how to work with someone when they are in the stress zone.

SONOMA *Waypoint Wisdom* 76:

If you want a longer life, do not count your days if you are nearing retirement. Rather, make your days count. Each day is an opportunity. Do not let Today's pain and Tomorrow's worry, take away any of Today's joy or Tomorrow's dream.

QR Code Express Conversations & Mind Exercises into...
Stress Releasers

Measure your performance and add scores to the PSCP Matrix at the end of the book

Personal Sonoma Colour Profile –
9: Measurement of Flow

Here is a simple way to measure your ability to deal with, and use stress effectively:

Answer Always, Sometimes, or Never

1. I see challenge as an opportunity to grow and develop.
2. I know when I am getting too stressed.
3. I know what to do before I get too stressed.
4. I know how to reduce stress when I feel Burn-Out.
5. I know how to be aware of stress signatures.
6. I know when I need more challenge in my life and work.
7. I know how to keep in Flow.
8. I know where to go for support when I need it.
9. I know where to go to support myself and/or my staff.

Scoring
Always = 3, Sometimes = 2, Never = 1

Sonoma Gold = 19-27
You are clearly in Flow and are more proactive than reactive to life's challenges. You are not afraid to ask for support and are very much aware of your own mental health.

Sonoma Silver = 10-18
You have moments of Flow interspersed with periods of

frustration and maybe a lack of progress. You might need to pay more attention to your mental health.

Sonoma Bronze = 1-9
Life can be a bit stop-start and almost like a grind at times. This situation is not sustainable. It is time for a self-audit to ensure you can proceed more effectively and healthily in the future.

Autumn Summary
The tide is turning, and it is turning rapidly, catching out both those who have become complacent and those who have stumbled. There is a harshness to the tide as it sweeps out to sea, leaving destruction in its wake. We must go with the tide, but we have learnt, and we know better how to flow with it, rather than against it.

The future might not be what we want, deserve or expect, but we have knowledge and experience, and our remaining journey may still hold some beautiful moments with an evergreen disposition.

So hold firm, embrace the next challenge of life, and be bold.

"Fall has always been my favourite season. The time when everything bursts with its last beauty, as if nature had been saving up all year for the grand finale." Lauren DeStefano (1984–present). American young adult author known for her *Chemical Garden* series and her gallows humour.

Winter

A Season when we are slowly losing our strength, but we may still have some laser influence, like a wise old owl circling its prey. In Winter we review our accrued knowledge and wisdom, utilise it and, if we are evergreen, we can add to our store.

We may feel a little more vulnerable in some ways, but we can still have a say in how the final Season pans out. We can stay curious, contribute and support others, and develop our capability for self-acceptance and gratitude.

We can salvage what we need in our ever-changing identity. We may even be able to secure new gains. But our physical ageing and growth is tapered and will diminish.

Winter is a time on your Sonoma journey to:

- Take stock of your physical and emotional health.
- Foster hope and recovery.
- Further develop integrity and humility.
- Reflect on your achievements and renew your aspirations.
- Be grateful you have got this far as many do not.
- Contextualise loss and disability.
- Create success and legacy.

We must search for any lingering opportunities still present. We must hope when we know it may be lost. Above all, we must remain true to whom we have become, and loyal to those who have supported us.

"I wonder if the snow loves the trees and fields, that it kisses them so gently. And then it covers them up snug, you know, with a white quilt; and perhaps it says, 'Go to sleep, darlings, till the summer comes again'." Lewis Carroll (1832–1898). English writer, logician, Anglican deacon and photographer. Celebrated author of *Alice's Adventures in Wonderland.*

Lesson 10:

La Dolce Vita – A Lived Sweet Life

Integrity & Humility, Hope & Recovery, Pain & Disability

Hidden Story – Dodgy Dave Learns his Lesson

Best friends, Dave and Harry were weight training in the gym and were resting between sets. Dave glanced up and saw a sign on the wall:

Integrity is something we do even when nobody is watching.

It started to make him think about his life and his recent actions in particular. Dave was a 'wide boy' who never missed an opportunity to make a fast buck, regardless of upsetting others in the process. In fact, he often bragged about some of his dodgy deals. 'All is fair in love and war' was what his father told him, and shown him! He was just a chip off the old block.

Only recently he had sold an unreliable car to a friend. Within weeks the car had broken down several times and his friend wanted a refund. Dave had a stock answer for him – *'Sold as seen, friend.'*

Dave never gave the transaction another thought.

On another wall in the gym was another sign. This caught the attention of Harry:

A great man is always willing to be little.

This sign resonated with him as his father had always told him that sometimes in life we have to be the bigger man, be humble and back down. Admit when we are in the wrong, and, temporarily at least, become the little man.

Thinking no more about the signs, both friends carried on with their lives, sometimes together, but increasingly apart, as their outlooks on life were beginning to differ significantly. As the years passed, Dave and Harry eventually went their separate ways.

'Dodgy' Dave had made a wad of cash selling cars from his 'two-bit' car lot. He continued to refuse any refunds and began to threaten some customers with a one-way ticket to the hospital and even sold fake goods to his girlfriend. 'Dodgy' Dave did not understand the words 'integrity' and 'humility' but idolised arrogance and ignorance. If he could get away with something, he would. He only knew how to play the big man.

'Humble' Harry had also become successful and knew how to make a fast buck. But his focus was not around money, or ripping people off. He preferred to provide honestly for himself, his work colleagues and to support the community. He regarded everyone on the same level, by being polite and courteous, often going out of his way to help others. Even though he was a successful businessman, he did not look down on anyone and could play the little man.

The old friends' paths were to cross again. It was a meeting that was to change Dave's life forever. After they had exchanged stories of what they were both up to, Dave started to get jealous of Harry's lifestyle. Harry explained about how being a little man from time to time helped him secure some big contracts and win over new friends. He was also using his money to support local charities.

Dave told Harry about how he was always looking over his shoulder for a disgruntled customer, who one day might be bigger and nastier than him. It was a lifestyle that was tiring, and it was catching up with him and affecting his health.

After the conversation Dave changed.

Over the next few months, Dave, recalling those two signs in the gym all those years ago, made it his mission to live up to integrity and humility every single day. It was a relief to come clean as he had become tired of being the bad guy all the time. 'Dodgy' Dave sold off his car lot and used some of the money to fund a new community centre for disadvantaged youngsters. At the opening of this centre, Dave received a compliment:

"Thanks, mister, we really appreciate your generosity and you looking after us by building a community centre. My dad calls you 'Dodgy' Dave, but I think I will call you 'Dependable' Dave."

The moral of the story is that we should be humble by respecting everyone and act with integrity in all our interactions and transactions.

P.S. A further example of integrity is the story of the old man who each day visits his wife in hospital. His wife has dementia and does not recognise him, but he still visits. When asked why he still visits her, his answer is one of true integrity:

"Even if she doesn't know who I am, I still know who she is and what she means to me."

Global Story – Terry Can Waite a Long Time for Hope

Terry Waite was the envoy to Robert Runcie, the Archbishop of Canterbury. As part of his remit, he was involved in hostage negotiations in the Middle East. His role was to secure the release of kidnapped prisoners. However, during a hostage negotiation to rescue British detainees in Lebanon in January 1987, he himself was kidnapped. He was kept in solitary confinement, forced to sleep on a floor chained to a radiator, in darkness for up to twenty-three hours a day. For up to an hour every day, he was beaten and subjected to mock executions.

After his release, he said he dealt with this situation by having positive thoughts:

"Keeping my mind alive and by keeping hope alive... I recognised that I still had a life, and although it was very limited, I was still able to live as fully as possible, living one day at a time."

He wrote many stories in his head, including one that would become his first book upon release.

He was constantly looking for sources of inspiration that would sustain him. He recalled that in the dark cell, a chink of light would come through the shutter on the window. Gradually that light illuminated the room, and he used this as inspiration:

"Don't give up, remember light is stronger than the darkness. That helped me maintain hope in that situation. My captors have the power to break my body, the power to bend my mind, but my soul is not yours to possess. My soul belongs to God."

After 1,763 days in November 1991, he was released. One of the lessons he learnt was that before he was captured, he had sympathy for those on the margins of life like the homeless, the prisoners, and other less fortunate people. Now that sympathy or pity for somebody, had changed to empathy, or real understanding for somebody. He considered that as one of the gifts from his experience (Wikipedia, Terry Waite).

My Story – Abridged Foray Into Ross World

This story is not going to be one of self-indulgence. Rather, it will highlight some challenges hopefully for someone else to connect with and maybe see hope in their own journey. Also, remember what I referred to at the start, that often comparisons are futile as they serve no real purpose.

For most of my life, I never really saw myself as someone who was less than anyone else because of my worsening disability and health. My mantra was to accept, push on and believe better days are ahead. To some extent I still do this, but in recent years things have changed significantly.

I often look at my challenges based around the age at which they first appeared. My 'challenge' timeline is *17, 24, 27, 51, 54, 61, 62*. Currently, a part of me still refuses to believe the following events have actually happened to me and I think that can be both good and bad.

At age *17* in 1978, I developed the usual acne, which failed to go away. In fact, with my intensive physical training at the time, my body went into meltdown. I was hospitalised for one month with acne covering nearly forty per cent of my body. I felt down, worthless and dejected with life. In fact, it has probably taken me over thirty years, with accompanying facial laser surgery in three countries, to not care anymore about parts of my body being scarred. On the plus side, it triggered my resilient attitude of proving people wrong, that I was worth something. This was heightened at the time by my exam failures.

At 24 in 1985, I incurred a torn anterior cruciate ligament (ACL) knee injury playing indoor soccer in Canada. It was an injury that required knee reconstruction in Toronto later that same year. At the time, this type of knee surgery was thought to be revolutionary. Sadly it wasn't.

Within twelve months I realised that I was not going to return to normal. I played one more soccer match in Saudi Arabia, but my knee could not cope, so I retired, aged 27, and a year later I could not run anymore.

I have since realised that this type of knee surgery, i.e. iliotibial band ACL replacement has become obsolete. As much as it gave the knee stability, it almost fast-tracked heavy arthritis in both the knees, and sadly, the ankle due to my changed gait. Over the years, I have had three further knee and ankle operations.

In 2012, aged 51, I was diagnosed with Peyronie's disease which made me feel isolated and detached.

Three year later, aged 54, I experienced over fifty episodes of high heartbeats, flushes, excessive hyperventilating and peeing that necessitated hospitalisation. At one point it was almost like an ambulance was permanently parked outside my house. It took a while to receive a diagnosis of panic attacks and I was adamant I would not take the

Citalopram (antidepressant medication) offered to me because I did not want to be hooked on tablets for the rest of my life and would rather have daily panic episodes than be 'weak'. That was the narrative of stigma running in my head. After three months I started to take the medication.

Nearly two years later, I eventually turned the panic attack corner and came off the medication.

In 2023, aged 61, I had a total knee replacement and got diagnosed with atrial fibrillation (AF) on the operating table. This is a condition where the heart beats erratically and can go over two hundred bpm – a normal resting heartbeat rate for an adult is sixty to eighty bpm. As a result of this, you are at higher risk of blood clots, stroke and heart attack. There are reportedly over one million people who experience this condition in the UK (Stroke UK). I am not alone. What differs is the frequency, intensity, and duration of attacks, as well as the diagnosis and accessibility to treatment.

The one consolation was that I received an immediate and accurate diagnosis that left undiagnosed could have been fatal. The downside is that I may have to wait two years for a treatment that only has a fifty to seventy-five per cent chance of success.

The knee recovery has been fraught with setbacks such as developing a post-operative pulmonary embolism (PE) and a new knee that distressingly clunks and clicks every time I move it. Sadly, the new knee alignment has made my ankle pain much worse, and has created new pain in my 'good' knee.

While writing this book, aged 63 in 2024, I am experiencing daily AF which means erratic heartbeats can confine me to a chair for hours at a time. The medications of beta-blockers and blood thinners slowed me down. So after six months, I decided to come off all medication, after persuading my GP this was the right course of action for me.

Further knee and ankle surgeries may be due, and in the meantime, I am having cortisone injections for my hip and ankle. This makes it difficult to work, and is a major reason I am writing this book… when my AF allows me.

How do I deal with this?

Sometimes poorly, with self-indulgence and far too many calories. For many years I was severely obese, at one stage reaching twenty-five stones (160kg). After recovering from my panic attacks, I eventually reduced my weight to fifteen stones (95kg) by changing my diet, eating less, and I began fasting. I started doing exercises that did not aggravate the knee and, crucially, I stopped drinking alcohol and I have been alcohol free since 2018.

Beyond this, I coped by distraction, a refusal to accept a medical label one hundred per cent of the time, an ignoring of what was really going on, plus a very liberal dose of inflated optimism and hope, along with a burning desire to prove people wrong. I still believe my best years are ahead of me.

Over recent years I have also had some purple patches, defying pain and joint mechanics, to fell walk for an hour maximum and I have been tearing up the gym on the good days. It may have caused some damage, and I may not fell walk ever again, but it was worth it for the vivid memories. Those days seem a long way off now.

How do I deal with this today after my recent diagnoses?

My knee, ankle and hip are crying out, *'pain!!!'* It is almost relentless. Nevertheless, I went to Booths in Fulwood, Preston, armed with my crutch to lean on, and a large dose of motivation. Almost immediately on entering the store, I realised I could not push a shopping trolley.

I sat on a stack of washing powder to catch my breath and relieve my pain. It came out of nowhere, but I started to well up. Hope for the future evaporated and I wondered how many more operations I would need. Could I ever get fixed, and be able to walk again, pain and limp free? I caught myself mid-catastrophisation and just avoided 'cripple crying'.

However, when I do get a window of pain relief, then more often than not, I experience an episode of AF. Such episodes can last from one to six hours. These episodes stop me in my tracks, and the way I deal with it is to sit down in a quiet environment and wait. It is like my 'challenges' are playing a tag-team strategy to take me down and they are top players!

On another occasion, I was meeting a friend, Stephen Toulmin, for coffee and my AF got a hold of me. For over an hour I sat in my car waiting for the beats to normalise. In the end, out of sheer frustration, I disregarded the AF, climbed out and took a few steps to the café (at the same Booths store). I could not make it and sat shaking on an outside bench to contemplate my next move.

An elderly couple noticed my plight and asked me if I was okay. There was really nothing they could do, but it was touching to be noticed. From experience, I know that an ambulance to hospital results in several hours of waiting under observation normally to be told to go home and see my GP… again! I called my friend to postpone our coffee and retreated back home to sit in my armchair for the remainder of the day.

Pain, AF attacks and frustration all seem to happen at Booths… I think I should shop somewhere else!

Coincidentally, I read about a trial by Liverpool John Moores University of 2,155 people who used customised shopping trollies to detect possible AF and two hundred and twenty shoppers were detected as having irregular heartbeats (*Daily Mail*, 2023). I think this is a smart move, as it was accompanied not only with an appointment with a medical professional, but also quick access to treatment and therapy.

In simple terms, it feels like I am living in the shadows, being semi-reclusive, and waiting for the next AF episode to present itself. I am trying to find a way to get back to the light again where I can be the authentic Ross, maybe a better version of Ross, richer for the experiences of my adversities.

If you have faced personal health challenges, how did or do you face these challenges?

What I have learnt about my challenges is that diagnosis is crucial, and treatment is critical. But treatment waiting lists are long and diagnoses may not always be accurate.

Interestingly, two high-profile AF specialists have questioned whether my previous panic attacks in 2015 were actually misdiagnosed, and in fact could well have been episodes of AF… don't you just love an accurate diagnosis?

Siege & Crisis States

When we know we don't feel well, I refer to this as Siege State and this can be amplified when we don't receive a diagnosis or understanding. Crisis State is where we need urgent treatment. We can also be constantly between Siege and Crisis.

Siege and Crisis states can often be found with conditions such as depression, panic attacks, and, as I have found, AF. The person needs medical assistance but also empathy – feeling with the person – and not sympathy, where pity is felt. Often when we do not receive this empathetic support in Crisis, that is the one thing that can torpedo recovery and even push us deeper into Crisis and beyond.

I have learnt the true value of receiving concern and unconditional support. If I feel my GP cares, it helps massively. If I feel my friends care, and demonstrate this, that helps massively. As we have seen earlier in Lesson 6, sometimes there may not be a fix to life's challenges.

This feeling of being listened to, for people to understand how you are feeling, and to show care and perhaps love, are qualities that can have a defining impact on a health situation. Simply feeling proud of staying in the battle, for me, should not be underestimated – it is an ongoing achievement.

"*What matters most is how well you walk through the fire.*" Charles Bukowski (American poet and novelist).

As we have mentioned before, sometimes humour can help. At my doctor's surgery recently, I was sat next to a friend who described the oncoming rush of aches, pains and disease within the age range of sixty to seventy. He described it aptly as Sniper's Alley. He advised me to just keep ducking and diving. The problem for me is that I am a bigger target!

Deep Dive – Hope & Recovery – We Must Believe

As we age, in the Winter of our lives, our bodies can start to inexorably deteriorate. What can we do to prolong longevity and health, physically, emotionally and mentally? What evidence is out there that we can use and take advantage of to increase our health span and life span?

We know that our emotional and mental health can impact our physical health, and vice versa. There is a symbiotic link between the two – one feeds the other. Research conducted by Mental Health First Aid England (2020) suggests that up to forty per cent of those with long-term clinical depression will experience forms of cardiovascular disease. Similarly, a University College London team working with a sample size of 670,000 over-forty-five-year-old subjects, found that depressed people are seventy-two per cent more likely to develop heart issues (*European Health Journal*, 2023).

But what is happening physiologically to our bodies when we either adopt a hope and recovery model, or when we adopt negative thinking and give up hope of recovery?

John Naish (*Daily Mail*, June 20th, 2023) looked at various studies around positivity, negativity and health. Dr Dang Wei, an epidemiologist at Karolinska Institute in Stockholm, observed how a broken heart actually breaks the heart. Individuals who lost a close family member had higher risks of atrial fibrillation, heart disease, heart attack, stroke and heart failure. This effect was especially heightened during the first week after loss, but can be a factor for years to come according to other studies (JAA Heart Failure).

Following up this link of emotion with negative physiological change was Hedva Hakin, an immunology researcher at the Technion-Israel Institute of Technology. She looked at a region of the brain called the ventral tegmental area (VTA) and its relationship with positive emotions and motivation. Through her research she noticed that when the VTA is activated (through positive thinking, motivation, etc) it triggers immune changes that help reduce damaging heart scar tissue.

Could this also apply to other parts of the body?

Dr Gabor Maté in his book *When the Body Says No* (2019) talks about how hope of recovery can greatly influence cancer recovery. In one study, looking at the impact of positive optimism on cancer, he discovered that in some of those patients who practised positivity, had support systems and had positive role models, the spread of cancer could be slowed and life prolonged. Interestingly, living alone had a shadow over it as many times this was a negative factor. If only on this evidence alone, should I invest in a partner?

Delving deeper into the word 'hope', we find it is regularly associated with the word 'recovery'. Often, people who experience mental health challenges talk about hope of recovery. On the MHFA training, we came across Dr Pat Deegan who experienced schizophrenia. In her initial diagnosis, aged seventeen, she was told that she was a 'schizophrenic' and 'schizophrenic people' do not recover and that she should retire from life. This language in itself is first-degree inappropriate labelling, stigmatising and does nothing to help the cause of those experiencing this challenging condition.

This diagnosis challenged her to fight her prognosis and eventually become a doctor who would fight limiting beliefs around schizophrenia diagnosis. It was this very belief that kept her going, a hope she held onto that she would live a fuller life, and that she could change the lives of others. She is living testimony that the power of hope can change lives.

There are other life cases where people have clung onto hope of recovery, or rescue. This very act or process has perpetuated their survival:

- Robert Bogucki survived forty days in the hot Australian desert.
- Lisa Theris was lost for twenty-eight days in isolated woods.
- Aleksandr Kovalev was lost in sub-zero temperatures for two weeks without food and water.

Deep Dive – Pain – is Painful Sometimes

But the good news does not stop there about chronic pain, i.e. pain that lasts for at least twelve weeks. Dr Cathy Stannard, a former pain consultant and clinical lead for NICE chronic pain guidelines (*Daily Mail*, June 2023), refers to Professor Gerald Zamponi at the University of Calgary (2020) who showed that the same ventral tegmental area (VTA) stimulation alleviated the condition of mice crippled with pain.

What was probably happening was the VTA, when stimulated, released the reward hormone dopamine into the pain-producing area of the prefrontal cortex. Often this area of the brain gets 'stuck', producing pain sensations. But when the VTA was stimulated it interrupted this negative cycle and pain levels subsided. Crucially, Zamponi believes motivation and positivity can also stimulate the VTA to transmit dopamine.

This viewpoint is not dissimilar to that of the National Institute for Health & Care Excellence (NICE). In 2021, NICE decreed that non-steroid anti-inflammatory drugs (benzodiazepines or opioids) should no longer be given as first-line treatment for chronic pain as there is little clinical evidence they work, especially long term, and could even cause more damage. Dr Cathy Stannard categorically believes that painkillers for chronic pain do not work and their side effects can do more damage:

"Medicines for pain relief may help at least in the short term, but there is evidence that suggests these become less effective over time, and can leave us with unwanted side effects such as brain fog, fatigue and weight gain."

The Cochrane Research Body also found that antidepressants do not work for chronic pain and a 2015 Australian study found paracetamol use was not effective for chronic pain relief.

Challenge

It is so difficult to be positive when you are in either Siege or Crisis states. If you believe that paracetamol for example, helps you, then keep taking it to get you through the short term. You just need to do, what you need to do, to overcome that peak pain period. People with pain know their own bodies and which routines work best for them. The only additional thing I would say is that trying different approaches to pain management can only be a good thing.

So where does that leave the patient?

We know that with chronic pain, there are other factors that amplify the pain such as depression, grief, fear and being in debt for example, and these can negatively influence brain chemistry, thus exacerbating pain. NICE, though, does recommend cognitive behavioural therapy (CBT) or acceptance commitment therapy (ACT) which aims to help patients replace negative thinking with positive ways of framing their lives and futures.

Backing up this point, a study by Imperial College London (2020) found that when chronic obstructive pulmonary disease (COPD) and heart disease patients received psychological therapies, they felt better, and as a result, their physical conditions improved, and in some cases, needed less medical intervention treatment.

A study by the Karolinska Institute in Sweden looked at the benefits of ten weeks of CBT with one hundred and twenty-seven AF patients. The aim was to change the way people thought and acted with this diagnosis. Early results did show that anxiety was reduced with a similar reduction in the need for care. This does not surprise me.

Often I can reduce and stop attacks, when I accept what is happening, and then embark on a complete distraction or adopt a belief that I am making progress. This happened a few weeks ago when I was having AF all day and my chair therapy was not doing the trick. At night I reluctantly attended a small Simon & Garfunkel tribute act gig in a local village hall. As soon as I arrived at the venue, my AF disappeared. There must be a cognitive component to AF – perhaps a 'Bridge Over Troubled Water'.

Dr Russ Harris (2011) advocates acceptance commitment therapy (ACT) which he uses to dampen down fears, and this in turn can have a dampening down impact on pain. Dr Harris says that we should learn to be with fearful emotions. By being present, we can take away some of the mystique of this dreaded emotion. I have adapted his theories into two thinking strategies which I have highlighted in the Mind Exercise at the end of this Lesson.

Can exercise help with pain?

University Hospital North Norway (2023) in a study put ten thousand people on light exercise. It improved pain tolerance, lessened pain and improved the quality of life. The 2021 Active Gloucester Scheme confirms this, that light exercise can only benefit pain management.

Can prosocial behaviours help with pain?

Interestingly, another way to lessen pain is via prosocial behaviours. Prosocial behaviour is the act of doing volunteer work, or simply donating to charity.

In a study by the University of London as part of UK Household Longitudinal survey (2011–2020), forty-eight thousand subjects with long-term chronic pain, who had become depressed and less motivated to exercise, were studied over nine years to see the impact of prosocial behaviours. Those subjects who donated to charity had reduced chronic pain symptoms, while those who actively pursued volunteer work, had even greater pain reductions.

Furthermore, a 2013 study by Arizona State University found that people over fifty-five who volunteered to help charities were twenty-four per cent less likely to die prematurely than those who did not volunteer. Even watching someone being altruistic can help the body fight off infections (Harvard University, 1988).

Can your diet help with pain and recovery?

I believe that having a 'healthy' approach to your diet can have so many benefits in terms of reduced pain, and a quicker, more sustained recovery. The problem is there is so much information surrounding food and this same information can be conflicting. From personal experience, when I indulge in a better diet, I notice significantly less AF episodes and my emotional state seems to be lifted and my low moods seem lessened. There is more positive consistency to my mindset.

Here are my ten golden food rules that really help me 'surf' above pain which sustains my optimism for the future:

1. Eat less. Eating less puts less stress on your digestive system.
2. Try fasting. Fasting gives your stomach and associated digestive organs a chance to reset and there is evidence out there that this fasting process can stave off disease. Common fasting periods are twelve to sixteen hours.

3. Try and make most of your meals yourself. Limit processed food and ready meals as these often contain ultra processed foods (UPF) ingredients which can be very harmful in many ways as they often contain 'food modifications' with higher fat, sugar and salt content

4. Avoid anything low fat or low sugar as these products often contain other ingredients which again can be harmful.

5. Eat your last meal of the day early. Try and eat at least four hours before sleep. I often finish eating by 5pm and I go to bed before 10pm.

6. Use a Nutribullet or blender. Getting daily raw and cooked vegetables enables antioxidants to work their magic on the body. These are crucial in pain management. Try and add a small portion of vegetables for breakfast!

7. Do a little research. Find out which foodstuffs help certain conditions, and which antagonise others.

8. Drink still water. Avoid any fizzy drinks, limit caffeine, reduce or eliminate alcohol and do not smoke.

9. Supplements. If you believe in them, then use them. Over the years I have used many, but what I try and do is have a period where I do not take any and then see how it affects my body and mind.

10. Moderation. Have your treats, as denial uses up finite willpower. But make sure the treats are very occasional.

A final food for thought from two historical erudite heavyweights:

"Let food be your medicine and medicine be your food."
Hippocrates.

"Take your food as medicine, or your food will become your medicine." Steve Jobs. Former Apple CEO.

Deep Dive – Disability – A Gift to Embrace or Pandora's Box?

Another thing I have found is that when we become disabled, it can isolate us. There are 17.7 per cent or 9.8 million disabled people in the UK in 2020/21 (Ons.gov) and there are eleven per cent disabled children, twenty-three per cent disabled working age adults and forty-five per cent pensioned disabled adults (Scope). These figures are on the increase, and as we live longer, more of us may have to deal with disability at some point in our lifetimes. But disability can also positively change your mindset. It can fire you up to fight and make gains in life that you previously would not have known possible.

TV celebrity Rose Ayling-Ellis, who has a hearing disability, suggests we should embrace our disability. I applaud this sentiment, and on occasions I can almost achieve this. But it is up to every disabled person to figure out what works best for them with their resources.

Could you embrace disability if you were disabled?

The resource of people is critical, i.e. having someone around who can understand you, emotionally lift you up, nudge you without judging you, is so underrated in terms of effective 'medicine'.

I think of disability as a Pandora's Box. Once it is opened up, there is no going back, so it is pointless going through all the *what if* scenarios, i.e. what if I had jumped out of the way of that sly trip while playing indoor soccer in Canada in 1985, or what if I had not gone to Canada. After my recent knee replacement, I wish I had not had it done. But Pandora's Box has been opened.

To avoid more pain, less social outings and less contact is better than enduring unwanted additional pain caused by such trips. Pain can also negatively change your mindset, impact your self-worth, and restrict opportunities for professional engagement. Some days it feels like I have aged twenty years ahead of my time. On other days, I believe I can fight the good fight.

Disability can also diminish you psychologically, and as we have seen, this can have a detrimental effect on our emotional and mental health. Often when people are in chronic pain, this can create depressive moods with outbursts of apathy and anger in equal measure. This pain state has the capacity to create clinical depression.

Be careful to watch out for this and seek professional and personal guidance, or at the very least, have those conversations with your support team, to tell them exactly how you feel. Being vulnerable and seeking support is a strength and never a weakness. Without putting too fine a point on it, vulnerability could save your life.

As we have mentioned in mental health in Lesson 3, writing things down can be beneficial to get a handle on the challenge. I went a step further, and made a mini-documentary about my challenges. It helped me get things out in the open and understand my challenges better (Ross, YouTube).

A health psychologist called Dr Ingela Thuné-Boyle

corresponded with me via email around a quote she had made about pain. The way she put it resonated with me:

> "*People don't often associate chronic pain with grief,*
> *but the realisation that life will never be what it was,*
> *and the future is not what you thought it would be,*
> *is a major loss.*"

Famous Example of Humility — The Two Sirs: Tom Finney & Garfield Sobers

Tom Finney was knighted in 1998 and I had the pleasure of announcing him onto the pitch at Deepdale soon after his knighthood was awarded. The crowd of over eighteen thousand was in full voice as they sung, 'One Sir Tom Finney, there's only one Sir Tom Finney!'

TV cameras were capturing the moment, and I was about to deliver a mini-interview with him in the centre circle. As we waited for the crowd's noise to die down, he turned to me and said something that was incredible:

"Is all that noise and clapping just for me?"

He was staggered by the response, and was so humble he even questioned whether he deserved it.

Another example of humility was demonstrated by Sir Garfield Sobers when I eventually met him at the National Football Museum in 2004. I was organising a meet and greet luncheon with Sir Gary and ex-footballer Duncan McKenzie.

I had worked with Duncan before, and he was always down to earth and friendly. But on this occasion, he was running late, and over one hundred diners were awaiting his arrival, and he was chauffeuring Sir Gary!

When they did arrive, almost an hour behind schedule, Duncan was apologetic and just wanted to catch up for lost time. He could not apologise enough for his lateness.

Sir Garfield, having seen the distress and impatience on the faces of some guests, caught the moment beautifully. He offered to sign any items of cricket memorabilia right there and then!

"Humility will open more doors than arrogance ever will." Zig Ziglar (1926–2012) American motivational speaker, author and salesman.

SONOMA Waypoint Wisdom 77:

Once we act with humility and integrity, life has a habit of repaying us and those close to us.

SONOMA Waypoint Wisdom 78:

Being humble more often will bring people closer towards you more often than any amount of egotism. Try and play the little man from time to time.

SONOMA Waypoint Wisdom 79:

When we find ourselves in desperate times, hope of recovery is maybe the only thing we have left. Hope can keep us alive. There are always stars in a black sky.

SONOMA Waypoint Wisdom 80:

Without diagnosis and a treatment plan, it may be difficult to have a consistent recovery.

SONOMA Waypoint Wisdom 81:

In Siege states, i.e. when we know we are feeling unwell, physically or mentally, with or without diagnosis, this is a time where understanding support can make all the difference to the person in this state. Crucial to this is the ability to open up to a non-judgemental person or persons who can then offer support.

SONOMA Waypoint Wisdom 82:

In Crisis states, i.e. when we are hospitalised, or need intensive treatment, you need people supporting you who understand the emotions you are experiencing. Hopefully, we are not in Crisis all the time, but people can judge you harshly when you are in respite, but show no symptoms of distress.

SONOMA Waypoint Wisdom 83:

Anecdotally, molecularly and physically, bearing hope and possibilities of recovery can positively impact disease. When this is allied to support systems and positive role models, recovery is more probable.

SONOMA Waypoint Wisdom 84:

If you donate to charity and actively volunteer to help others, there is a likelihood that your pain levels will subside. If you volunteer, or even watch altruistic acts, this can reduce your odds of premature death.

SONOMA Waypoint Wisdom 85:

Disability can isolate people and it can even make people angry and depressed. Try and find ways to be positive and enlist a team of loyal and understanding supporters.

SONOMA Waypoint Wisdom 86:

Recovery might not take us to a place that was the same as before illness. Recovery may not be perfect or linear in time, as each person may recover at a different rate. Keep believing that there are better days ahead.

QR Code Express Conversations & Mind Exercises into...
Surfing Above the Pain Wave

Measure your performance and add scores to the PSCP Matrix at the end of the book

Personal Sonoma Colour Profile –
10: Measurement of Qualities & Skills

Here is an adapted questionnaire to measure integrity, humility, aspects of hope, optimism and supporting others:

Answer Always, Sometimes or Never

1. Do you do what you think is the right thing even when nobody is watching?
2. Can you play the little man from time to time?
3. Do you stick to your values and beliefs when they are being actively challenged by others?
4. Do you behave with integrity around different groups of people?
5. Can you see hope in most situations? Do you believe that some form of recovery is possible?
6. Do you look for the positives of a situation?
7. Do you support friends who really need support?
8. Do you support relative strangers?

Scoring
Always = 3, Sometimes = 2, Never = 1

Sonoma Gold = 19-27
You are someone who is very positive and can relate very strongly and empathetically to others and their needs. You

are humble with a high degree of integrity and people will know this about you.

Sonoma Silver = 10-18
You lean towards positivity in most scenarios but lack a consistency in your approach. You have qualities of integrity but can give out mixed messages. You are a good friend to others, but can you do more?

Sonoma Bronze = 1-9
You have some degree of positivity and are able to support others. But do you have a consistent motivation and desire to do this? Do people question your integrity from time to time?

Lesson 11:

Winter's Flowering Perennials

Renewed Aspiration & Reinvention, Reflection & Feed-forward, Expediency & Facilitation

Hidden Story – Winter Breeze Jasmine in my Mind – Be More Like Eddie & The Stones

A keen gardener, old Eddie went to survey his garden first thing every morning. He liked this time of day, as it was not only peaceful, but he could see changes in his garden, even though it was Winter.

He noticed the continued withering of plants, flowers and weeds, slowly returning to the earth. But now and again, one often referred to as the star jasmine (*Trachelospermum jasminoides*) would surprise him. Eddie had planted this shrub for many years as they are perennial plants, and its leaves could survive in Winter too.

This Winter was no exception. It was like seeing himself as a mirror image of the jasmine. He was in the latter stages of his life, but had not thrown in the towel just yet. He was still keen to learn and apply new and old knowledge, to any particular challenge that occurred.

Eddie had seen many of his friends pass away, and many had almost given up on life before their time was up. Eddie did not judge his friends, but he was determined to keep pushing forward, taking on new challenges and learning new skills. It was almost like the jasmine, when it flowered in Winter, was a signal to Eddie, for him to renew his aspirations in life.

What Eddie did not fully appreciate was that he was actually inspiring other friends, and even strangers, to renew their aspirations too. His optimistic attitude was contagious. Some of his friends also started to plant star jasmine and when they flowered in Winter that was a reminder to them to renew their own hopes for life. They nicknamed him Evergreen Eddie.

The weeds would come back in Spring and Summer, and even Autumn, but the Winter was the Season of the evergreen star jasmine.

Like the star jasmine, there are evergreen performers in life, who may be at the end of their careers or even at the end of their life, who continued to flower in their Winters:

- Novak Djokovic, Rafael Nadal, Roger Federer, Serena and Venus Williams.
- Mick Jagger, Willie Nelson, Dolly Parton, Dionne Warwick, Tony Bennett.
- Sir Alan Sugar, Joan Bakewell, Kris Jenner, Betty White, Stan Lee.

Global Story – 'Aaay' The Fonz, Betty is All White & Susan is a Jewel

Being able to reinvent ourselves might be a key trait that distinguishes the 'has-been' from the 'new breed'. There can be a tendency in later life, to kick back and enjoy the fruits of our labours. There is nothing wrong with this viewpoint. But keeping a renewed purpose in life, by possibly reinventing ourselves, may yield a richer life.

The following examples are of people who have successfully reinvented themselves:

- He starred in *Happy Days*, one of the most famous American TV sitcoms of the mid-seventies – eighties. But after the show ended, he struggled to find work as he was typecast as The Fonz. After some short-term cameo appearances in movies, and nearly fifty years later he started to find acclaim once again on TV with the comedy series *Barry* (2018–2023), which earned him an Emmy Award.
- He has also written the popular Hank Zipzer children's book series about a boy with dyslexia after he himself was diagnosed with dyslexia (Wikipedia). His name is Henry Winkler.
- She was a successful and well-known actor who continually changed her career path in radio, film and TV, appearing in sitcoms (notably *The Golden Girls*), movies, game shows and hosting shows. She had many firsts including first female to produce a sitcom, and first to receive the Daytime Emmy Award. She received awards up to just before her death aged ninety-nine in 2021 (Britannica.com). Her name is Betty White.

- When she was growing up she wanted to be a fashion designer, but in her era, women's opportunities beyond family were almost frowned upon. So she married, had a family and became a homemaker. She worked occasionally in retail in the Summer for her husband's family business.

After divorce, and with the children grown up, she had time, freedom and ambition. She decided to make jewellery and upskilled herself by taking many classes to learn the skills needed. Eventually she was proficient enough to sell privately to family and friends, and then sell to the public through an upmarket Nantucket shop in Boston's Museum of Fine Arts. At the same time she sold real estate to earn income to sustain her dream.

The collapse of the real estate market in 2008 pushed her to pursue jewellery making exclusively full time. At aged sixty-nine, she opened her first shop. She has developed her niche in the market with vibrant, organic, wearable jewellery that reflect her love of the sea and nature (Covey Club). Her name is Susan Lister Locke.

My Story — Canada Calling for Elite Performers

Many educationalists, including Barry Hymer and John Hattie, whom we referenced earlier, believe that our greatest learning can come through reflection. The Education Endowment Foundation found that there are over forty ways in which learning can be improved. But in terms of time and cost to implement, feedback and metacognition reflection (thinking about thinking) rate amongst the most effective.

Having talked previously about feedback, I want to introduce a relatively new concept of feed-forward and link this to reflection. In simple terms, feed-forward is where we troubleshoot what is going to happen in the future. We try to map out what the future holds before we encounter it.

Metacognition reflection is where we think of different ways we can reflect on events to maybe improve performance in the future.

A silly example of this might be a crossword challenge against a friend. Once completed, you might review the clues you answered, and how they might have helped or hindered your opponent. Could you have spent more time working on an answer using a variety of memory techniques, or even slowed down to activate different parts of your brain, in the hope of an inspired answer? Did you avoid the clues that you immediately felt were too hard, but on seeing the answers, did you recognise the answer was within you? This is metacognition reflection.

Professionally, I have come across both feed-forward and metacognition reflection in my extensive time within education. Whilst studying for my master's degree in Canada in 1984, the course of Sports Coaching Theory & Practice would make me aware of many aspects of performance. This involved understanding disciplines associated with elite performance such as psychology, biomechanics, physiology, social dynamics, nutrition, etc. The essence of the course was to understand where the gains could be made in terms of elite performance.

There is a temptation in sports coaching to be very didactic and just keep giving the athlete instructions about how to improve performance. There is a place for this, but I believe it is *after* you have allowed the athlete to think through their performance (like Tim Gallwey in Lesson 6), both *before* it has happened and *afterwards*.

Through feed-forward techniques, we observed experienced coaches asking swimmers what were the barriers to shaving off milliseconds. Answers varied.

Once all the answers were collected, the coaches then used *Guided Learning* (giving clues and support) and *Open Questioning* (looking for more detailed and specific answers) to solicit further examples of areas to be improved or directed to look back on their original answers.

The whole point was to let the swimmer be an integral part of the learning process. If they owned this process, there was more chance they would believe the recommendations and put these into practice with one hundred per cent motivation. We are only talking about 'marginal gains' here, but a few milliseconds, or millimetres could be the difference between success and failure, gold and silver.

It was no surprise to anyone on the master's programme, that many athletes made significant marginal gains that allowed them to access greater national funding for their sports and so compete on a bigger stage. Four of the athletes in our cohort went on to win Olympic medals.

Have you ever used metacognition and feed-forward and did these processes work for you?

Deep Dive – Feed-forward & Reflection – The Dragons & John Harvey-Jones are Trouble... Shooters!

Feed-forward processes can be seen on *Dragon's Den* where inventors ask for investment from the Dragons. Often they are quizzed didactically with closed questions (directly telling and asking for knowledge) about their finance projections to see if the product or service is worth investing in.

Similar to this, if you are around my age, were the exploits of entrepreneur John Harvey-Jones in the ground-breaking BBC TV series *Troubleshooter*. I had bought his eponymous book and read it from cover to cover, and was fascinated. He would go into failing businesses and suggest ways of turning them around. This was an outstanding example of reflection and feed-forward. However, he did not always get it right. In one episode he told Morgan Motor Company to cease trading as it could not be successful. The same company is still trading today!

Boris Takes Bobby's Bait – Check Mate for The West

Perhaps the best example of reflection and feed-forward comes from the world of chess. At around the age of eleven, I got interested in chess, until my twin kept beating me, then my best friend Graham beat me. I quickly realised I was not going to be a Grand Master. But something about the game got me hooked and that feeling still remains to this day.

To be a Chess Grand Master you must be able to look into the future moves for yourself and your opponent, and learn from your ongoing and post-match mistakes. Believe it or not, there are 2,026 Grand Masters. But perhaps the most famous of these were Bobby Fischer and Boris Spassky who met at the 1972 World Chess Championships in Iceland.

Spassky was the current world champion and known as a ruthless player, who would often use psychology and surprise to outwit his opponent on the chessboard, and away from it.

Fischer was more erratic in his outlook on life. He had a phenomenally high IQ, yet was often insecure and had extreme views. He even threatened not to attend the Championship, and, when he did attend, he was late.

During the matches, Fischer would sacrifice pawns to see the reaction of his opponent. Spassky's previous reputation for being over-expansive and aggressive in his playing style, was what Fischer was trying to exploit to his advantage. But, leading into the game, and with a new coach, Spassky was more considered in his approach.

Fischer would also not go for short draws or quiet draws where a match would be tied early on. He wanted to stretch Spassky in any way he could. This included changing his usual opening moves. In the end, Fischer was triumphant and became the first naturalised American to be crowned world champion.

A Grand Master like Bobby Fischer or Boris Spassky, or maybe all of the remaining 2,024 Grand Masters, had to have a strategic feed-forward and reflection overview. It has even been suggested that many can think out twenty-five to thirty moves ahead of their next move (Chess.com, 2018).

So, whether you are involved with educating people, an elite athlete, a failing business, a hospitality company or a chess prodigy, to be successful, and sustain this success, you will need feed-forward and reflection.

Deep Dive – Expediency – Chairman Bryan is in Charge, but Teachers are Not

As we enter our twilight years, some things become clearer to us. One such thing is that time is very precious, and we need to utilise it very carefully, with expediency, i.e. acting efficiently, practically and effectively with an end in mind.

This can be a much sought-after quality, and when applied correctly, to the right situation, with the right 'on-side' personnel, it can yield results. For example, previously around the table of a board meeting at PNEFC, I have witnessed expediency. Often it is wrapped up in a tight agenda that always finishes on time, with definite allocated timed slots to feedback and a concise summary. A future plan of action is agreed with specific responsibilities.

Bryan Gray, a former successful chairman at PNEFC, was a stickler for expediency in terms of time and relevant information. I learnt so much from him when he was chairing our heads of department board meetings. He was a sublime businessman who could cut to the chase in terms of rational detail. He just wanted the bottom-line figures from each department and a very brief forecast. He certainly did not want any excuses, no matter how true or valid they were.

However, expediency might not always be the way to proceed in all cases. Expediency can manifest itself as getting the job done, at all costs, no matter what the collateral damage. The end justifies the means?

In one particular large secondary school in Blackpool, I witnessed an expedient unilateral senior leadership team policy that all parties had to adopt, with no questions asked, with no prior staff or parent consultation, and with a pinch of threat and menace. It was not long before various parties started to challenge the wisdom and effectiveness of this policy. After several revisions, and still no consensus, the assistant Heads made the right expedient decision – to bury the policy.

Have you ever employed expediency above empathy? If so, did you encounter the outcomes you desired?

Facilitation – Face to Face or Online but Don't Attempt the Temple Pose

This next skill might just be the most important skill that you have at your disposal. Unfortunately, not many people have been trained in this area and fewer still therefore utilise it well. This skill is facilitation.

The Association for Talent Development defines facilitation as:

"The act of engaging participants in creating, discovering, and applying learning insights."

In applied terms, this could mean creating an open, honest and trustworthy environment where everyone and their opinions feel valued and appreciated. This environment, if created well, will also foster a gentle challenging or confrontation of views without upsetting or closing down people. There should be a 'rules of engagement' agreement that values everyone's opinion, promotes inclusivity and diversity and in an atmosphere that feels safe.

When achieved and done implicitly and subtly, facilitation empowers the stakeholders to fully own the process. In essence, it builds greater participation, alignment and allows full unfettered expression. This can mean better outcomes. Facilitation clearly has its seat in empathy, which we covered in Lesson 6.

The role of the facilitator is to do all of the above, but when needed, guide people back to the agenda, softy enforce the terms of engagement and ultimately, steer the group to the desired outcomes.

I have witnessed good facilitation, and sadly, have been a perpetrator of poor facilitation.

I was once in a meeting with Paul Heathcote, the celebrated chef and restaurateur and I was talking about a particular problem that needed solving. When I had finished speaking, Paul suggested a solution. In very poor facilitation style, I instantly rebutted his suggestion, and said we had already tried that.

What I could have said, with a much softer tone, and gentler phrasing was:

"Paul, you think the same way as me on some things. I have tried that possible solution, but it didn't work for me. Can you expand on it to see if together we can make it work second time around?"

Facilitation can often revolve around a single word or concept. In years gone by, I was knowledge-hungry, i.e. to give it out or to highlight it from delegates.

Someone would mention a word or concept, and you might feel intimidated that you do not know what it really means, or you do know, and you do not give the person credit. So, rather than say:

"Yes, that's all well and good, but…"

We should say:

"I like that word/concept, in fact I'm going to use that in my next training session. Can I have your permission?"

Or:

"That sounds interesting, can you explain that idea a little more?"

Deep Dive – Facilitation – Richard Askam is the Perfect Facilitator, Jenny & Oshor are Super-Facilitators & Mindset Don Lifts People

A couple of years ago I had the pleasure of hosting BBC sports journalist and presenter Richard Askam in an executive box at PNEFC on a match day.

I knew Richard was a solid media professional, having done the hard yards studying journalism before finding his natural place in front of the live cameras. What I didn't know, was that Richard is an expert at facilitation, and ipso facto, empathy.

When any guests asked Richard any questions, he was polite. But beyond this, he was genuinely curious about others. More often than not, after answering a question, he would enquire about the person asking the question, asking about their opinion or simply asking them what was their profession.

He expertly and authentically facilitated the conversation so that people felt important and included. What really made it authentic was the congruency of his words, with his body and facial language – you couldn't fake that.

Two other people I have had the privilege to know, and work with over time and call friends, are Jenny Pelling and Oshor Williams. These people possess what I call super-facilitation, which embodies validation and empathy seamlessly linked to expediency, attention to detail, and reflective skills. This super skills combination usually makes someone feel important and empowered for positive sustained change.

How do they do this?

I have known Jenny for about three years in her role as director of apprenticeship development and diversity at Kaplan (a company which provides training and apprenticeships in accountancy, data, tech, and financial services). We work together to deliver monthly Mind Fitness webinars to apprentices.

Jenny and colleagues analyse feedback from apprentices to devise a schedule to meet learner need, and we do this well in advance, so we all know where we stand in terms of content and delivery dates.

Jenny always invites me to share my knowledge, asking what would make appropriate content. When I show her the draft versions, of which there may be a few, she has a nice knack of pointing out the good stuff, but gently asking if there is another way of highlighting a point or replacing a point or theme, and often through a series of questions rather than didactic demands.

I can't tell you exactly how she does that, all I know is it just works for us and she makes me feel empowered and validated. Jenny draws on her vast experience to see the bigger picture of the webinar product and understands how to ensure all participants are included.

Jenny constantly reminds me that we can often get further in life by asking questions that are held in empathy.

Oshor Williams is a former professional footballer and currently holds the office of assistant director of education with the Professional Footballers Association (PFA) where he provides advice and guidance to players preparing for life after football.

I have known Oshor for over thirty years and our relationship started when he had the bravery in his position as community development manager at PNEFC, to allow a large limping referee to officiate a half-time match on the hallowed turf of Deepdale in the 1990s, all in the name of charity.

Since this time, our paths have intersected socially, and at times, professionally. What has always struck me about Oshor is his forensic attention to detail and his openness to share knowledge and skills. He constantly validates you by engaging in authentic conversations and never fails to mention your own qualities and achievements. He is a reflective thinker which has been borne out over the years with his academic achievements post-playing career and his elevation to a well-respected part of the prestigious PFA.

However, for me, the one quality that stands out is that

Oshor is the epitome of seeing the best in everybody. This is why many people are irresistibly drawn to him.

In a nutshell, what Jenny and Oshor have in common is that they make a person feel validated and empowered, with no direct reference to their own skills and knowledge – they are understated super-facilitators.

I encountered a final example of facilitation linked to inspiration when I recently had a telephone conversation with previously mentioned elite mind coach, Don Macpherson.

Don offered his time freely to me, even though I was a stranger. From the get-go of our thirteen-minute telephone conversation, he was more interested in me than talking about himself.

At the end of our conversation I asked him for some words of wisdom from him, as a successful professional with nearly seventy-five years on the clock, to me, a sixty-three-year-old who was still trying to figure out life. His words were immediately impactful and left me feeling validated, important and hopeful:

"Keep going, keep helping others: maybe you can't help everybody, but never forget to help yourself as this will help you help others, this is selfish, and it is a necessary quality. You may be twelve years behind me, but I believe there is so much more to come from you, Ross."

He is an authentic expert in lifting people up, maybe lifting them higher than they believe themselves. His impact on me was immediate, and I believe it will be permanent.

Deep Dive – Online Facilitation

Over the last few years, with the proliferation of online training, I have witnessed poor and excellent facilitation.

The secret is to get to know your delegates online, and show an authentic interest in them. By knowing them better, you will also notice their skillset and knowledge base, and you can use this during the course. Being authentic, or real, is having my camera on when I am a delegate, and as an instructor, making people feel valued by noting everyone's comments, verbally or in the chat box.

A good online facilitation is about managing the breakout rooms, so that all people have the opportunity to share views with each other. This approach also breeds greater collective knowledge.

It is so tempting when you are delivering accredited courses to stick rigidly to the exact formula in terms of timings, content, elaboration of concepts, etc. But if you are too expedient, trying to get to an agreed end, you might miss the chance for greater engagement and facilitation, which could result in not only enhanced learning, but also more enjoyment.

Good facilitation involves being authentic or real. That comes through active listening, using non-verbal cues like nods, and 'ums' to allow the talker to explain their opinion. It also comes through not showing any bias or using distracting behaviours, words or non-verbal actions that detract from a person's concentration or a group's progress.

I have often seen facilitators adopt the Temple Pose where they sit with elbows on the table, and their hands placed in a praying position just touching their chin. It might look like they are thinking, but many body language experts, such as Allan and Barbara Pease (2017) think this can be interpreted as condescending. In short, try and not touch the face for any length of time.

Movement around a room, spending time with different individuals and groups, can also aid greater trust through showing closer proximal interest. Equally, asking permission to make notes, or even being the official note-taker in a meeting, shows your willingness to do tasks not normally associated with your position. It is an endearing quality that builds better facilitation.

Personalise responses and choose different adjectives to compliment or challenge comments. Otherwise you become the teacher who says the same thing to everyone and eventually nobody listens to that teacher.

Always give people time to process information, because once you lose someone, they may not be willing to catch up, especially if you are unaware that they are behind. A good facilitator always checks for individual learning.

Do not be scared of confrontation, especially if this is done with softness and curiosity as this can often lead to clarity and agreement, and an even closer bond.

Challenge

You must be authentically interested in the people, the process, and the outcome. If this is not the case, no amount of 'clever' facilitation you employ will help you deliver on a project effectively. Personally, facilitation starts with knowing people's names and ends with agreed objectives met.

Famous Example of Facilitation – Roman Abramovich, Jose Mourinho & Joe Cole

Chelsea had won another Premiership title after beating Bolton Wanderers 2-0 in 2005. The whole team and entourage had returned back to the Marriott Hotel in Preston to celebrate. This is where I came across Roman Abramovich, Jose Mourinho, Joe Cole and a couple of very hefty bouncers.

Not lacking any shyness, but being polite, I approached Roman and Jose, asking them to sign some football shirts which I always carried in the boot of my car for occasions such as this.

The two bouncers took a step forward, but immediately Roman waved them back. He and Jose were hospitable as they facilitated my request with smiling faces. Five minutes later, I was back with a handful of tissues and beer mats to sign, having run out of football shirts.

I had also been asked by a friend to ask if his young son could meet the two and get a photo with them. Again, nothing was too much bother. In fact, they asked his dad to join the photo opportunity and even invited us to sit down with them and ask any questions. They could not have facilitated us any better.

Later when I went to the toilet, I bumped into footballer Joe Cole. He did not mind signing his own shirt and giving it to me. It was pure facilitation and generosity, rather than being intimidated by a tall, heavy, limping man in the toilets!

Yes, I know they were all celebrating a famous title, but they went out of their way to be courteous and engaging. Top professional facilitators.

"If I speak of myself in different ways, that is because I look at myself in different ways." Michel de Montaigne (1533–1592). French author, philosopher and statesman.

SONOMA Waypoint Wisdom 87:

We all have something to give in life, no matter how old we may be. Aspiration may have served us well in our early professional careers, and it may continue to serve us well in our latter years. In fact, it could even keep us alive. Be more star jasmine.

SONOMA Waypoint Wisdom 88:

You do not have to be a celebrity or a top businessperson to take advantage of reinvention. Reinvention can work for anyone as it enriches lives and creates a renewed purpose.

SONOMA Waypoint Wisdom 89:

Feed-forward and metacognition are skills that can be used at any stage of ordinary life. As we age, and harness our experiences, our ability to be insightful can be enhanced by troubleshooting ahead of a challenge and reflecting after a challenge. This will allow us to respond more effectively next time.

SONOMA Waypoint Wisdom 90:

Feed-forward is an important tool if you want to keep evolving. A little foresight goes a long way in many businesses and within our personal lives.

SONOMA *Waypoint Wisdom* 91:

If you are not feed-forwarding the future or reflecting on the past, then you are planning for failure.

SONOMA *Waypoint Wisdom* 92:

Expediency can give us the outcomes we desire. Used in the wrong way, it can take us further away from our goals. When blended with authentic facilitation, positive results become inevitable.

SONOMA *Waypoint Wisdom* 93:

A great way to develop facilitation is to ask more questions than to make demands. This is linked to asking for permissions.

SONOMA *Waypoint Wisdom* 94:

Good facilitation comes from adopting active listening and using inclusivity to take everyone's views into consideration, whilst keeping on track to deliver the stated outcomes.

SONOMA *Waypoint Wisdom* 95:

Good facilitation is always about the process, valuing people and being authentic. If you get that right, you generally get the outcomes.

SONOMA *Waypoint Wisdom* 96:

Great facilitation is when you see the best in everybody... and often those people return their best. This is the classic Covey win-win.

QR Code Express Conversations & Mind Exercises into...
Thinking Ahead & Remembering Behind

Measure your performance and add scores to the PSCP Matrix at the end of the book

Personal Sonoma Colour Profile –
11: Measurement of Qualities and Skills.

A test for your ability to use expediency, facilitation, reflection and feed-forward abilities:

Answer Always, Sometimes, or Never

1. Do you possess the traits of supporting and guiding without an ulterior motive?
2. Do you ensure the process is fair, everyone has a voice, and people are included?
3. Do you know when to use expediency and when to use slower facilitation?
4. Do you think and reflect regularly after an event?
5. Do you feed-forward and troubleshoot every upcoming event?
6. Do you trust in a process by establishing agreed rules, standing back and supporting from the sides?
7. Do you empower and facilitate staff to reflect and feed-forward?
8. Do you authentically compliment staff, leaders and groups?
9. Do you ask more questions than make demands?

Scoring
Always = 3, Sometimes = 2, Never = 1

Sonoma Gold = 19-27

You are a person of principles and standards. People gravitate towards you, and you are consistent in everything you do and how you treat people. You are a good planner and don't cut corners and you aways try and finish any task in the right way. When things go occasionally awry, you reflect to ensure it doesn't happen again.

Sonoma Silver = 10-18

Generally you get the job done and carry people with you. You can be indifferent at times but are aware of this trait. You try to support others but sometimes frustration rules and it's all about getting the job finished. You can engender support and carry the group.

Sonoma Bronze = 1-9

You are seen as a team player and a likeable leader when things go well. There may be an inconsistency about you when things falter, and you see the end as justifying the means which could mean collateral damage to reputations and feelings.

Lesson 12:

Time Immemorial

Grief & Loss, Perspectives on Life & Death,
Succession & Legacy

Hidden Story – Jonny & Jenny React Differently to Bruno

Twins, Jenny and Jonny really liked their primary school. They did fun activities, learnt interesting facts about the world, the teachers were patient and kind, and they had lots of friends. While Jonny continued to thrive at school, recently Jenny seemed less energetic and happy as she once was. Something had changed, but her teachers and friends did not know what. Sometimes Jenny would be happily playing with her friends, but would then go quiet and a little distant, preferring to play on her own for a while.

Sometimes, Jenny would get upset when her best friend was absent, or when she had to speak in front of the class. At other times she would become angry at the smallest of things and would write on desks, or tear out a few pages of her exercise book. Of late, she was stopping behind after school, reading books on her own, while Jonny went home alone. It all came to a head when a teacher asked her why she had been nasty to one of her friends.

Before she could answer, Jenny burst into tears:

"Whatever is the matter, Jenny?" asked her teacher.

"Miss, I have been so sad recently. Our pet dog Bruno died a few weeks ago, and I can't stop thinking about him. I miss the fun we had together."

"Poor Jenny, why didn't you tell me sooner?" enquired the teacher.

"I didn't want to bother anyone. Besides, Jonny seemed okay about it, and I want to be strong like Jonny."

The teacher sat down with Jenny and started to explain something to her:

"We can all deal with loss in different ways. Some people can just move on like Jonny, and simply accept the situation. Others like yourself may think about losing Bruno and feel sad. I know other people who have lost pets and have gotten over the sorrow by getting another pet, while others want to talk about their loss. We all react in different ways – there is no right way to respond to losing a pet."

Jenny's mood lifted a little as she thought about what her teacher had just said:

"Shall we ring your parents to pick you up and while we are waiting we can chat more. You can tell me what else you have been thinking and doing to get over Bruno."

It took a while, but eventually Jenny came to terms with losing Bruno. With the support of her teachers, friends and her parents, Jenny was able to see other ways to think about Bruno's passing. Jonny even asked her to talk to him in future when she was sad.

Challenge

In 1969 Elisabeth Kübler-Ross devised a model to explain the Five Stages of Grief somebody goes through when diagnosed with a terminal illness.

The Five Stages are: Denial, Anger, Bargaining, Depression and Acceptance (DABDA)

Yet it has often been interpreted too literally, and each person's journey may be different in terms of phases and magnitude of associated emotions. Today the Kübler-Ross Change Curve has also been used to explain change and loss in a wider context beyond grief and death. (Kübler-Ross, 1997).

Global Story – Different Perspectives on Death

There can be many perspectives on death. Even though it comes to everyone, we can interpret the process differently. Which in turn can influence how we look at life.

The Dalai Lama talks about death in the following way:

"As a Buddhist, I view death as a normal process, a reality that I accept will occur as long as I remain in this earthly existence. Knowing that I cannot escape it, I see no point in worrying about it. I tend to think of death as being like changing your clothes when they are old and worn out, rather than as some final end. In life, I want to live fully, embracing its great beauty and pleasures. In death, I want to activate a virtuous karma in which I will be reborn." (AZ Quotes).

There are other examples from around the world, where people have been given a terminal diagnosis, and then started to think and act differently about their impending demise.

Susan Briscoe had just turned fifty, and was fit and healthy. But a routine doctor's appointment ultimately led to a diagnosis of terminal cancer. She came to terms with this situation quickly, as time was of the essence. She talked straight to her parents, her two boys, and her partner, telling them that she would be okay.

She talked about the imposters of loss and grief, and refused to entertain them. Instead, she started to focus on the flipside of grief, which was gratitude. With little else going for her, she could decide her emotions. When she felt grief, she made sure it was fleetingly, and then she chose to focus upon gratitude and joy:

"As much as my dying meant tremendous loss, it also meant receiving gifts of unimagined beauty and joy and love, not just for me, but for my loved ones too. Death has shown me that when I am living the life I am meant to live, I am giving."

By giving, Susan Briscoe meant that she had time to give to her family, to give to her community, to give to her teaching profession and give to her friendships (Susan Briscoe.com).

Dave Ismay, a comedian, spent his life savings after doctors told him he only had three months to live. He was so devastated by the initial diagnosis that he set out to complete his own 'bucket list' and achieve his lifelong dreams. This list included writing a book about close friend and fellow comedian Bob Monkhouse, playing golf at an exclusive Irish golf course, visiting Australia and appearing in a pantomime.

The sixty-four-year-old grandfather, who had performed both on stage and on television, had been told by doctors that alcohol abuse had left him with cirrhosis of the liver after test results showed he had excess iron levels. He was baffled because he had not been a big drinker and had cut down smoking when he was forty:

"When you're told you've got three months to live, it really focuses your mind. I even bought a new Merc because I thought, 'If I'm going to go, it will be in a comfortable car!'," Ismay said.

Eight weeks after his diagnosis, and after splashing out forty-six thousand pounds on the new Mercedes, Ismay underwent a full body scan test which showed he was in fact suffering from the non-life-threatening blood condition known as haemochromatosis. Fifteen months after Ismay's ordeal began, he published a book about Monkhouse and appeared in Redditch Palace Theatre's production of *Mother Goose*.

The thought of death really focused his mind and made him stop procrastinating about all the things he wanted to do. There was a clear change in his approach to life and he had more gratitude (*Independent*, 2013).

On this theme of terminal diagnoses, I came across a news article on a remarkable man called Simon Boas who had imminent terminal throat cancer (*BBC News*, July 4th, 2024). The headline to the article was:

'I'm as happy as I've been in my life.'

This immediately grabbed my attention, and as I read the article I had many thoughts... he's only young at aged forty-six, why is he so upbeat, and why is he spending his last few months writing a book entitled *A Beginner's Guide to Dying*?

He explained that he had spent much of his working life as an aid worker and had been surrounded by death and dying, often within cultures that were seemingly more accepting of this fate, almost to the extent that it is normalised... death is a part of life.

He had also been a Samaritan where he had listened to people in dire circumstances – this was an aspect of his life that he had become familiar with.

What really surprised me was a lack of self in his diagnosis. His thoughts were with his family and thinking about how they would cope when he had gone.

I don't think there would be many people who could possess this acceptance attitude.

Listening to Radio 2, I came across the wise words of celebrated musician Chrissie Hynde, Status Quo rocker Francis Rossi, actor Joanna Lumley and broadcaster Kaye Adams.

Chrissie Hynde talked about how, given she is in her seventies, she has started to embrace and enjoy her later years. Gone is the ego of being the best band in the world, playing the biggest arenas. Now she and her band prefer the clubs where there is less financial reward, but a more intimate and personal feel to connecting with an audience. She has embraced her age, has looked for joy at every opportunity and categorically states that the age she is now, represents the best part of her life!

Francis Rossi, also in his seventies, extolled the virtues of smaller, more intimate gigs. In particular, it allowed him to be his imperfect self, and he could make mistakes and even draw attention to them, rather than hide them and worry about them happening again. He now fully enjoys showing his authenticity, and this has come with age.

Even actor Joanna Lumley, who is approaching her eighties, says that death is normal and even suggests we should talk about death as if it is our friend... but we don't want it to become our friend too soon, let alone our best friend!

Kaye Adams has always been a go-getter and hard worker, having this work ethic instilled in her from her equally hard-working parents. However, at sixty, she said she is working less and less intensely. She is starting to learn how to really enjoy and savour life with a better blend of work and play. She described this shift in thinking:

"Stop climbing the mountain and admire the view."

I would rather be in this camp, as opposed to the camp of thinking about the Sword of Damocles, a looming danger of imminent death hanging above my head every day until the day it does finally drop.

Others, being more curious about how people perceived them, and maybe a morbid fascination to see their own death, have decided to arrange their own funerals, like a fake funeral.

Zhang Deyang was sixty-six years old when he decided to stage his own funeral. He arranged it himself, wondering how many would turn up given that he had never married and had no children. There was a particular reason for his concern – in Chinese culture, the dead are said to have needs, and their graves are supposed to be visited regularly to ensure those needs are met. On the day, forty invitees turned up at Deyang's funeral. Yet he was unhappy: twenty relatives and friends did not show up:

"I can't believe so many relatives and friends don't care about me," he was quoted as saying. (Daily Telegraph, 2016).

In 1997, Serbian pensioner Vuk Peric posted a fake death notice in his local newspaper, and sent invites for his funeral. He then watched the event from a distance, eventually emerging to reveal that he was, indeed, alive. He thanked the mourners for attending and received a very mixed response! (Mental Floss).

In 2023, David Baerten, a Belgian TikTok creator with over 165,000 followers, arranged his own funeral, and got his wife and daughter to post false death messages to make it seem more authentic.

He did the fake funeral to teach his wider family and friends a 'life lesson' about staying in contact with one another, insisting that you should not have to wait until someone is dead to meet up with them. It was his way of working out who really cared about him. In the end, only about half his family showed up. However, of the ones who did not show up, at least half of those have been in touch since. (*Sky News.*)

Another way to look at death is to view it with humour, as was the case with Spike Milligan, a legendary comic, playwright and poet.

A quote that is commonly attributed to him shows his mirth at death:

"I'm not afraid of dying, I just don't want to be there when it happens."

He lived to age eighty-three.

Finally, if you want to get close to death, why not try what the TV host, broadcaster and singer, Alexander Armstrong did? On a trip to South Korea he was intrigued about what happens inside the Death Experience School. He was invited to adorn a shroud before lying in a coffin. The coffin lid was then nailed shut. Then he was asked the question:

"Who is crying for you?"

Alexander Armstrong was actually in floods of tears himself, as he thought about all his loved ones. The experience certainly changed his outlook not on death, but on life.

Two more pertinent questions might be:

1. How big an opportunity now is there to enjoy your life without restraints?

2. How long will this window of opportunity be open for you?

My Story – The Books are the Legacy for Dad, Mum & Danni

My life changed forever on May 2nd, 2012, when my father, Bob McWilliam, died aged eighty-three. In fact, it changed when he received his terminal diagnosis in August, 2010. Between those two dates, I was relearning what it meant to be a son to the person who had the greatest impact on my life.

On August 25th, 2012, my young niece, Danni, died unexpectedly, aged just twenty-one. She was so full of life and did not let her special educational needs diagnosis hamper her – if she wanted to do something, or even say something, she would.

After several years of suffering with dementia, my blessed mother, Wyn McWilliam, passed away on May 23rd, 2017, aged eighty-seven. Like my father, she had always supported me, but often I was either far too busy or engrossed in my own challenges, to realise the depths of her support and love.

These three events have shaped my life. They have made me introspective, questioning my abilities, contributions and attitudes to those who gave me life and nurtured me, and those who added to my life.

Kübler-Ross and CBT have helped me understand the stages of my own grief, and its impact on my own health. It has been a long, difficult journey that has no end in sight at the moment.

One thing I have done to assuage this pain has been to write, and write I did. It was my therapy. During this time, I made a promise to honour them via the creation of my books.

My first three books were published in 2017, five years after my father passed away, as a tribute to him. It probably took so long because I was in various stages of grief and wanted to 'do him justice'.

My fourth book was published in 2019 to remember my mother and my fifth book was published in 2021 to raise awareness of special educational needs for my other niece, Alex.

This book you are reading is my sixth and still represents my attempts to articulate my promise to my parents. It is based on the fact that they supported and nurtured me unconditionally. They allowed me to study, grow and develop without any pressure or expectation. That promise is to reach my potential and support others in any way I can. It will drive me until the day I die.

By writing, I am creating my Legacy to my parents and young Danni. Through the books they will not be forgotten. I am also delivering on my promise when I speak or train people.

What I have become more acutely aware of, especially as I have encountered poor health, is to try to see and enjoy the moments, and not think too far ahead.

What do I mean by this?

I know it is something of a cliché, but try and see the good moments of each day, those 'magic moments', which we mentioned in Lesson 9. If it only breaks up that negative subconscious narrative, then it is a good thing indeed.

Firstly, on each day, I try and let the joy in. I even start off with 'let's see what the day will bring'. Believe me, some days are harder than others, but I try and do this. A big reason for this is that it breaks up my negative subconscious thoughts around my illnesses, and by doing this, I believe I have less pain and less AF attacks.

Secondly, I try not to think too far ahead these days,

as my very intense imagination fast-forwards to my final years and my mind paints a dismal picture. By just keeping focused on now, I can strike the right balance of reality and optimism. I am still aspirational, but I am also much more flexible in my approach to my aspirations.

Finally, I managed to see the 'joy in now' recently when I was speaking at an independent school in Leicester. After completing a forty-five-minute speech about how to develop children, a young child, maybe aged eight or nine, burst through the crowd of people surrounding me and asked if he could buy one of my books:

"Which book would you like?" I asked softly, holding up my three main books.

"It doesn't matter really," was his curt reply.

"Okay, how about *CUPPA*? Do you want me to sign it and put your name on the inscription?" I asked.

His response was immediate, unforgettable and priceless:

"No, that's okay, mister. My mum says that when people sign books the price goes down if they're not famous. It also means we can't re-gift it!"

Deep Dive – Legacy

Legacy is commonly defined as either:

1. A sum of money or property left to someone in a will
2. A long-lasting impact of events and actions. This could be nomenclature, ownership and permissions associated with buildings, literature, works of art, etc.

Deep Dive – Living Legacy

Imagine you are one hundred years old, and you are on your deathbed. All your family are around you, plus your good friends. Start to imagine all those people right now. See their faces and how they are acting and talking. Now, imagine you are about to die, and you only have ten seconds left on earth. The clock is ticking down… ten, nine, eight, seven, six, five, and as it hits five you have five seconds to tell the crowd of people your last words.

What are your words?

More often than not, when we are put in a situation like this, our last words are not only meant for our family and friends, but also meant as words of advice for ourselves. What are those words of advice for yourself as these could just be directly related to your Living Legacy?

Deep Dive – Famous Legacies

Famous and highly influential people have often left different, but impactful Legacies (Famous Legacies: Thrive Global):

- **Albert Einstein** (1879–1955) creating the Theory of Relativity, being a Nobel Prize winner and discovering the Law of Photoelectric Effect.
- **Martin Luther King Jr** (1929–1968) leading the USA Civil Rights Movement and delivering the 'I Have A Dream' speech to two hundred and fifty thousand people in 1963 in Washington DC.

- **Mother Teresa** (1910–1997) a legacy of selflessly dedicating her life to care for lepers, homeless and dying in the slums of Kolkata, India. Nobel Peace Prize recipient and canonised as Saint Teresa.
- **Nelson Mandela** (1918–2013) fighting for equal rights in South Africa, being imprisoned for twenty-seven years, defeating Apartheid, Noble Peace Prize recipient.
- **Marie Curie** (1867–1934) pioneering research into radioactivity which was to help the treatment of cancer, Nobel Prize recipient two times.
- **Agatha Christie DBE** (1890–1976) left a legacy of sixty-six books and fourteen short stories, whose works are still being enjoyed today.

It might also be an interesting idea to really galvanise our thoughts on Legacy, if we fast-forward to five years after you died and think about these questions below:

Five years after your death, what, if anything, will those beyond your family remember you for? _____ .

If you had to give everything you own to a cause (not a person), what cause would that cause be? _____ .

If your Legacy were to create a charity foundation, what would it be? _____ .

If you could snap your fingers and acquire an experience or talent in my Winter, it would be _____ because _____ .

By thinking ahead of ourselves, much like feed-forward in the last Lesson, we can start to get a clearer picture of our Legacy right now.

⬦ *The key question, though, is very simple: how do you want to be remembered?*

As for a Legacy after I pass away, it might look like a foundation supporting others, with my 'son' Ryan, having a role somewhere.

I also adore the phrase 'I have lived and won' and it is something I really want to be able to say with one hundred per cent authenticity at some point, in many, many years' time.

Deep Dive – Succession – Brothers in Arms, Moyes & Fergie

Often linked with Legacy, is the concept of Succession. Who is going to take over from you, in business, family matters, your social side and in your community responsibilities?

I was talking to my friend Peter Chester the other day, and he was recounting a story of a business that was going through the process of Succession. The company had been established over fifty years, and the founding partners, two brothers, wanted to step away and let their respective families run the business.

Plans were made to share business power with a child from each of the two brothers. Both children were to work together to take the business on to the next level, i.e.

modernise it, improve productivity, look for new services and products, and review personnel.

These were significant changes, and very quickly resistance was felt across the workforce. Not many people like change and this was certainly true with the staff. However, the clear lack of knowledge and experience of the two children made this transition impossible. Some staff decided to leave, while others confronted the children on almost every aspect of the proposed changes. Within weeks, the business was in disarray and close to closure.

What happened next?

Both brothers returned to the business for an agreed period of time to develop transition. Both children were given less responsibilities while they 'learned on the job' and were mentored by the two brothers. Two experienced staff members were promoted onto the board of directors. Eventually, the staff got used to the new way of operating and within a few months both brothers did manage to retire.

If you are in a similar position in business, then it might be a very good idea to think about transitioning sooner rather than later. This earlier approach will give you time to develop a pipeline of talent, to clarify the communication processes around company direction, ambition and staff opportunities.

A powerful example of poor succession occurred with Manchester United and manager, Sir Alex Ferguson. After joining in 1986, he eventually won thirteen Premier League titles, five FA Cups, four League Cups, two UEFA Champions League... and many more awards.

In 2013 he decided to leave, and his exit was very quick, giving the club publicly at least, just months to replace him. David Moyes stepped into that role, perhaps without much transitional handover. Maybe there was an assumption that Manchester United could carry on winning with almost any manager?

Without a real succession plan in place, David Moyes lasted just ten months. Successive managers have not fared that much better, and I wonder if an earlier and more sustained transition to a new manager and staff would have given them better outcomes since Sir Alex Ferguson left?

Famous Example of Legacy – It Ain't Half Hot, Windsor

Back in 1978 I was on a day trip to London as part of an annual WR Tuson College 'educational' visit. A group of us did a few touristy things and then I got led astray as we entered a Soho bar.

The place was very busy, and it seemed a good idea at the time to join my friends and have a pint of London Ale, or whatever it was called at the time. To my surprise and delight, sat right next to me at the bar was one of my father's favourite actors – Windsor Davies.

I initiated a conversation along the lines of 'My father thinks you're amazing in *It Ain't Half Hot, Mum*,' which was a popular sitcom in the 1970s. He was very engaging, and even asked me about my favourite TV shows, and what music my father liked, as they were from a similar era. I later found out they were born just two years apart.

I don't know why, but the conversation got onto careers, legacies and death. He said he just wanted to make people laugh and maybe that would help people forget about their problems for a while. He loved TV mainly because he could reach a big audience, and he had also made some amazing friends at the time through TV, such as Don Estelle and Melvyn Hayes.

He said that one day, when he was out of the spotlight, and in his failing years, he wanted to live overseas and watch the shows where he made people laugh.

He died in France, aged eighty-eight in 2019.

"It's very important that people know that I really enjoy everything that has happened to me. And tell my kids... you're not going to be the tallest, fastest, prettiest, the best track runner, but you can be the nicest human being that someone has ever met in their life. And I just want to leave that legacy that being nice is a true treasure." George Foreman (1949–present.) Former world champion boxer, entrepreneur, minister and author.

SONOMA Waypoint Wisdom 97:

By sharing our emotions, trusting in others and being patient, we can understand why we act in different ways when we lose someone we love. There is no correct way to respond to loss, there is no timescale and there should always be no judgement.

SONOMA Waypoint Wisdom 98:

The journey through the stages of grief may not be universally the same and recovery may not be linear. People can relapse back into previous stages. This further supports the concept that we can deal with grief in different ways.

SONOMA *Waypoint Wisdom* **99:**

Your perspective on death may influence your approach to life. When many people have faced imminent death, they seem to develop a greater capacity for gratitude.

SONOMA *Waypoint Wisdom* **100:**

The thought of death can focus the mind and may well reduce or eliminate any procrastinating.

SONOMA *Waypoint Wisdom* **101:**

Our perspectives on death can differ significantly. Perhaps we should concentrate more on life, and see what we can do with it and how we can help others in that process of living.

SONOMA *Waypoint Wisdom* **102:**

As we age, our one true commodity is time. We must try to use it effectively, productively, altruistically and joyously.

SONOMA *Waypoint Wisdom* **103:**

A Living Legacy really focuses your mind about your purpose in life right now.

SONOMA *Waypoint Wisdom* **104:**

Legacy is the way you made people feel and their memories of you. Was I a good person, did people trust me, was I patient with people, was I kind and generous, did I have the courage to be vulnerable?

SONOMA *Waypoint Wisdom* 105:

Succession planning might be something we need to consider for business and family affairs. Rather than wait for a crisis, put the necessary procedures in place that sees transition, that fuels the pipeline of talent.

QR Code Express Conversations & Mind Exercises into... Legacy and Which Animal are You... Really?

Measure your performance and add scores to the PSCP Matrix at the end of the book

Personal Sonoma Colour Profile –
12: Measurement of Life & Legacy

Try these six simple questions based around Loss, Gratitude, Legacy and Succession:

Answer Yes, To Some Extent or No

1. In the current Season of your life, can you flip the coin and see more gratitude and goodness?
2. Are you aware of how people's emotions and behaviours may vary around loss?
3. Do you implement strategies for professional succession?
4. Are you actively creating your Legacy?
5. If you retired tomorrow, would you feel fulfilled?
6. Do you think about how a pipeline of talent or support could benefit you and others?

Scoring
Yes = 3, To Some Extent = 2, No = 1

Sonoma Gold = 13-18
You can see the bigger picture and are actively pursuing goals for yourself and others. You are empathetic to loss and are creating future plans with and without yourself.

Sonoma Silver = 7-12
You are aware of the future changes that might lie ahead but you have a tendency to ignore or delay decisions around this. This approach was probably successful in your earlier life, but it needs to be softer and more adapted now to take into account the needs of others.

Sonoma Bronze = 1-6
You ignore the changes in life and are not responsive to others' needs. You have a tendency to bury your head in the sand and just keep pressing onwards. Now is the time to reset your compass of life.

Winter Summary
The tide has turned stealthily and is now far away. It has inexorably left us and abandoned us. We are high and dry. All that remains is the strewn debris in its wake. Our journey is coming to an end, and it is a time for a tallying up of our efforts, intentions and outcomes. Our fateful future might not be what we want, expect or deserve, but we have knowledge and experience, and our remaining journey may still hold some beautiful moments if we have hope and an evergreen disposition.

Our Legacy comes into clear view as we pass over the baton of responsibility. The end is always next to the start. So the start of your next journey, to an unknown destination, is waiting in the wings.

"Spring passes and one remembers one's innocence.
Summer passes and one remembers one's exuberance.
Autumn passes and one remembers one's reverence.
Winter passes and one remembers one's perseverance."
Yoko Ono (1933–present.) Japanese artist and activist.

Epilogue

We are closing in on the end of our journey together. Clearly, you have shown a high level of dedication, application and resilience to stick with the book.

As always, I am hopeful that you have now added some more tools to your Mindset Toolkit, with both Deep Dives of Knowledge and Sonoma Waypoint Wisdoms.

It is time for a period of reflection, and this is where you can collect your thoughts, consolidate your learning and reflect on all the positive things you have done, are currently doing or are going to do.

It may also be a time to jettison some of your bad habits, now that you have become more aware of them.

So, reflectively, *what has this journey together through the four Seasons revealed for you?*

REFLECTIVE *Waypoint Wisdom* 106:

Be more reflective about your journey through life.

- Indeed, be more conscious about your use of time. With time in mind, the idiom below is clearly appropriate: 'It's later than you think.'

(?) *So, why not use this book to kick-start your intent to maximise your use of time?*

REFLECTIVE *Waypoint Wisdom* 107:

It is important to have goals and ambition in life, in each and every Season.

- Often when we lose aspiration, time can catch up with us more quickly than we can ever imagine.
- Goals and ambition give our life purpose. When purpose is missing, we can drift and become isolated.

(?) *What are your goals and purpose, and do they need redefining?*

REFLECTIVE *Waypoint Wisdom* 108:

Do not end up with regrets, or a feeling of unfinished business.

- Can you make sure that your best years are still ahead of you to fulfil your potential?
- Or indeed, are they already behind you, creating guilt and remorse?

(?) *What can you do today to limit or banish regrets?*

REFLECTIVE *Waypoint Wisdom* 109:

One of our biggest fears is getting older – embrace this opportunity.

- As you age, do you want to simply implode and give way to illness, insular emotions and behaviours?
- Or do you want to counter this, and keep challenging

yourself, to keep believing that positive things will happen and be strong as you age?

- Optimal management of your emotional and physical health can increase both your health and life span.

(?) *Are you embracing ageing, or are you denying it?*

REFLECTIVE Waypoint Wisdom 110:

If you are going through pain, or even illness, then please try and keep hope.

- When you are in the 'eye of the storm' life can seem pretty worthless, like a challenging phase that will never pass.
- Life is all about phases, so each phase will pass eventually.
- The outcome might not always be perfect, but it will pass.

(?) *Do you have more strengths than you know?*

REFLECTIVE Waypoint Wisdom 111:

Value yourself and do not compare yourself – always.

- Continually endeavour to value your own self-worth. Otherwise, a compromised position evolves. It's an easy trap to fall into.
- Believing that others have much more to give than yourself, prevents you from developing your own high value stock.
- Equally, judging your success negatively by the financial success of others is a futile exercise. Success is measured in many ways.

- Remember, everyone has something valuable to offer.

❓ *What do you have to offer?*

REFLECTIVE *Waypoint Wisdom* 112:

Go with the Flow.

- Through the decades, you have gained more knowledge and experience than you will ever appreciate.
- Occasionally, be prepared to accept more and sometimes allow life to deal up what it will – go with the Flow. It will serve you well in the long term.

❓ *When did you last demonstrate Flow?*

REFLECTIVE *Waypoint Wisdom* 113:

Slow down... so you can speed up?

- This might sound counterintuitive, but slowing down can actually increase focus and prioritisation, ultimately resulting in greater effectiveness and impact.
- Many successful people do not go fast all the time, some avoid this state.
- My father often compared me to the former F1 driver, Stirling Moss, when he quoted "Slow down, Stirling, you will get there, it's not a race."
- One of my favourite phrases is 'It's not always about getting there first... just as long as you get there.'

❓ *In what area do you need to slow down?*

REFLECTIVE Waypoint Wisdom 114:

Be prepared to show vulnerability.

- Having worked with, and alongside, many top professionals, the ones that stand out are those that have the capability to demonstrate appropriate vulnerability.
- Nobody knows it all, or has the perfect response to every situation. Recognising this, and demonstrating vulnerability, can go a very long way to endearing support, building trust and empathy – all crucial leadership traits.
- So rather than appearing 'weaker', vulnerability can make you 'stronger'.

When was the last time you showed vulnerability?

REFLECTIVE Waypoint Wisdom 115:

You will find your way Home if you look in the right places.

- Whether we fully know it or not, we are searching for our Sonoma Home.
- A homely place where we feel secure and can reflect on our achievements, a place where we can share our lives with those closest and dearest.
- A place of work where we feel professional with a capital P and a feeling that we are nestled perfectly where we rightfully belong, where we have reached our potential.
- A place where we can support others, and help others reach their potential.
- This book, and the Sonoma Lessons, may at the very least, make you aware of this. At its best, you will arrive Home.

⟨?⟩ *Will this book ignite you into action?*

REFLECTIVE ⟨*Waypoint Wisdom*⟩ **116:**

It's nice to be nice.

- You will probably be remembered for your acts of kindness, especially when people really need that kindness, rather than any professional achievement.
- Spread kindness far and wide, to friends and strangers alike. Life has a funny way of repaying us, often when we least expect it.

⟨?⟩ *When were you last nice to a family member, friend, colleague or stranger?*

Epilogue Story

There was a man who had four sons. He wanted his sons to learn not to judge things too quickly. So he sent them each on a quest, in turn, to go and look at a pear tree that was a great distance away. The first son went in the Winter, the second in the Spring, the third in Summer and the fourth in the Autumn. When they had all gone and come back, he called them together to describe what they had seen.

The first son said that the tree was ugly, bent and twisted. The second son said it was covered with green buds and full of promise. The third son disagreed; he said it was laden with blossoms that smelt so sweet and looked so beautiful and it was the most graceful thing he had ever seen. The last son disagreed with all of them; he said it was ripe and drooping with fruit, full of life and fulfilment.

The man then explained to his sons that they were all right, because they had each seen but only one Season in the pear tree's life. He told them that you cannot judge a tree, or a person, by only one Season and that the essence of who they are and the pleasure, joy and love that come from that life can only be measured at the end, when all Seasons are up.

If you give up when it's Winter, you will miss the promise of your Spring, the beauty of your Summer and the fulfillment of your Autumn (Creative Youth Ideas).

If we interpret this as a once only cycle of Seasons, as we have endeavoured to do with this book, then we may indeed judge Winter as ugly and bent with no hope or Summer as beautiful and everlasting. Yet, each Season always offers an opportunity especially if we view it in a continuous yearly perspective.

In fact, it is often not what happens to us that is important. It is more about how we interpret these events and take meaning from them. So, take meaning from each Season and apply it to your life, no matter how long you perceive you have left. With this in mind, always bear hope no matter whatever Season you find yourself within.

Personal Sonoma Colour Profile Overall Matrix (PSCPM)

Sonoma Score Each Chapter	Colour
1	
1	
2	
2	
3	
4	
5	
6	
7	
8	
9	
10	
11	
12	

Personal Sonoma Colour Profile (PSCP) Matrix

Gold – You are perfectly nestled in your rightful Sonoma place. Life feels good and all your efforts and achievements are bearing fruit. Your challenge now is to maintain this Sonoma feeling for the years ahead.

Silver – Good consolidation of your Sonoma place. Still a little way to go yet, but you are on the right track. Be patient, keep applying yourself and you will soon arrive at Sonoma.

Bronze – Lots of opportunities to improve, so keep having belief that soon you will see the benefits of your endeavours. Sonoma is waiting for you. Don't let the opportunity slip by.

GOLD

SILVER

BRONZE

Place your Sonoma scores in the diagram

References

Introduction

Covey, Stephen R. *The 7 Habits of Highly Effective People* (2004) Simon & Schuster

Wikipedia Sonoma Origins (2013) https://en.wikipedia.org/wiki/Sonoma_Valley

Lesson 1

Dweck, Carol S. Mindset: *The New Psychology of Success* (2006) Penguin

Hattie, John *Visible Learning* (2008) Routledge

Ricci, Mary Cay *Mindsets In The Classroom: Building A Growth Mindset Learning Community* (2013) Prufrock Press

Adapted Popular Mechanics 2017 https://www.popularmechanics.com/science/animals/a25814/riddle-of-the-week-21/

James Altucher, Wikipedia https://en.wikipedia.org/wiki/James_Altucher

James Altucher Daily Practices https://jamesaltucher.com/blog/how-to-be-the-luckiest-guy-on-the-planet-in-4-easy-steps/

BBC: *Gods of Tennis* https://www.bbc.co.uk/sport/tennis/65501241

Lesson 2
Green, Charles H. & Howe, Andrea P. *The Trusted Advisor Fieldbook*
Johnson, Spencer *Who Moved My Cheese?* Vermilion Press
Terry Fox Foundation
https://terryfox.org/terrys-story/
YouTube Colin Powell (2011)
https://www.youtube.com/watch?v=IfL3RSa5T5Y
Steve Jobs
https://www.psychologytoday.com/gb/blog/cutting-edge-leadership/201202/why-steve-jobs-is-a-leadership-nightmare
Tim Cook Wikipedia
https://en.wikipedia.org/wiki/Tim_Cook
Simon Sinek
https://www.mjpeople.nl/en/simon-sineks-key-to-successful-leadership-in-the-hospitality-industry/

Lesson 3
Buckingham, Marcus & Clifton, Donald O. *Now Discover Your Strengths* (2001) Free Press
Syed, Matthew. *Bounce: The Myth of Talent and The Power of Practice* (2011) Fourth Estate
Mental Health First Aid Training Materials (MHFA 2020)
https://www.journal-advocate.com/2013/10/11/a-tale-of-two-brothers-and-a-secret-you-must-know-about/
Dementia and Music – Walsh, Causer & Brayne (2019)
https://pubmed.ncbi.nlm.nih.gov/31814445/
Arnold & Meinhard Schwarzenegger
https://www.distractify.com/p/what-happened-to-arnold-schwarzenegger-brother

Lesson 4

Buzan, Tony *The Memory Book: How To Remember Anything You Want* (2009) BBC Active 1st Edition

Covey, Stephen R. *The 7 Habits of Highly Effective People* (2004) Simon & Schuster

Heath, Chip & Dan *Switch: How To Change Things When Change Is Hard* (2010) Random House

Elton John

https://www.independent.co.uk/arts-entertainment/music/news/elton-john-glastonbury-setlist-full-b2364134.html

Don Berwick

https://en.wikipedia.org/wiki/Donald_Berwick

Alexander Pan July 2015 Ten Movies That Had Insane Attention To Detail Whatculture .com

https://whatculture.com/film/10-movies-that-had-an-insane-amount-of-attention-to-detail

Cliff Young Wikipedia

https://en.wikipedia.org/wiki/Cliff_Young_(athlete)

Lesson 5

Hansen, Rick *Resilient* (2018) Rider & Co

Hardy, Darren *The Compound Effect* (2010) John Murray One

Alexander, Mariam *The Guardian* newspaper (March 1st, 2021)

Lesson 6

Carnegie, Dale *How to Win Friends and Influence People* Republished (2019) Vermilion

Colombus, Katie *How To Listen* (2021) Octopus

Heath, Chip & Dan *Switch – When Change Is Hard* (2011) Random House

Scott, Susan *Fierce Conversations* (2003) Piatkus

Sarah Willingham, BBC Business News, November 2022 https://www.bbc.co.uk/news/av/business-63457629

Verywell Mind, May 2023 https://www.verywellmind.com/what-is-emotional-intelligence-2795423

Paul Ekman https://www.paulekman.com/universal-emotions/

Michael Parkinson – BBC News https://www.bbc.co.uk/news/entertainment-arts-66411604

Meg Ryan Interview https://www.thesun.co.uk/tv/23530516/sir-michael-parkinsons-frosty-chat-meg-ryan/

Lesson 7

Black, Don *The Sanest Guy In The Room* (2020) Constable

Brown, Brené *Braving The Wilderness* (2017) Random House

Covey, Stephen R. *The 7 Habits of Highly Effective People* (2004) Simon & Schuster

Macpherson, Don *How to Master Your Monkey Mind – Overcome Anxiety, Increase Confidence and Regain Control of Your Life* (2021) Penguin

Phelps, Michael https://www.yourswimlog.com/michael-phelps-visualization/

Yeung, Rob *Confidence: The Art Of Getting What You Want* (2008) Pearson Life

Ross, Granada TV

https://www.youtube.com/watch?v=6bfSYerQ8w0&t=3s
Schwarzenegger, Arnold *Be Useful: Seven Tools for Life* (2023) Penguin

Lesson 8
The Dearing Review 1994 http://www.educationengland.org.uk/documents/dearing1994/
Harland Sanders Wikipedia
https://en.wikipedia.org/wiki/Colonel_Sanders
Taisto Miettinen
https://en.wikipedia.org/wiki/Taisto_Miettinen

Lesson 9
Crum, Alia Mindset Matters: *How To Embrace The Benefits of Stress* podcast (September 16th, 2021)
https://www.gsb.stanford.edu/insights/mindset-matters-how-embrace-benefits-stress
McGonigal, Kelly *The Upside Of Stress: Why Stress Is Good For You (And How To Get Good At It)* (2015) Avery
Selye, Hans *The Stress of Life* (1978) McGraw-Hill
Hachikō *BBC News* report July 1st, 2023
https://www.bbc.co.uk/news/world-asia-65259426
Maté, Gabor *When The Body Says No* (2019) Ebury Publishing

Lesson 10
Harris, Russ *The Confidence Gap: From Fear To Freedom* (2011) Robinson
Maté, Gabor *When The Body Says No* (2019) Ebury Publishing
Mental Health First Aid Training Materials (MHFA 2020)

Terry Waite, Wikipedia
https://en.wikipedia.org/wiki/Terry_Waite
Office for National Statistics
https://www.ons.gov.uk/
    peoplepopulationandcommunity/
    healthandsocialcare/healthandwellbeing/bulletins/
    disabilityenglandandwales/census2021
Scope
https://www.scope.org.uk/media/disability-facts-figures/
Ross, YouTube: Challenges Interview
https://www.youtube.com/
    watch?v=s98lKip9MUo&t=318s
John Moores AF Trial – Rachel Ellis, *Daily Mail*, August
    22, 2023
https://www.ljmu.ac.uk/about-us/news/
    articles/2021/5/17/can-supermarket-trolleys-help-cut-
    risk-of-stroke--trials-underway
Daily Mail, CBT AF Study Karolinska Institute
https://mailonline.pressreader.com/
    article/282226605272861

Lesson 11

Pease, Allan & Barbara *The Definitive Book Of Body
    Language: How To Read Others' Attitudes By Their
    Gestures* (2017) Orion
The Education Endowment Foundation
https://educationendowmentfoundation.org.uk/
Chess.Com 2018 Spassky v Fischer 1972 World
    Championships
https://www.chess.com/article/view/fischer-vs-spassky-
    world-chess-championship-1972

Henry Winkler
https://en.wikipedia.org/wiki/Henry_Winkler
Betty White
https://www.britannica.com/biography/Betty-White
Susan Lister Locke
https://www.coveyclub.com/blog_posts/reinvent-
    yourself-10-women-who-did-it/

Lesson 12
Covey, Stephen R. *The 7 habits of Highly Effective People*
    (2004) Simon & Schuster
Kübler-Ross, Elisabeth *On Death and Dying* (1997) Simon
    & Schuster
Dalai Lama
https://www.azquotes.com/author/8418-Dalai_Lama/tag/
    death
Susan Briscoe Website
https://susanbriscoe.wordpress.com/tag/gratitude/
Dave Ismay, *The Independent*
https://www.independent.co.uk/news/obituaries/dave-
    ismay-obituary-entertainer-who-was-wrongly-told-
    he-had-three-months-to-live-8659896.html
Simon Boas
https://www.bbc.co.uk/news/articles/clmykzrdnljo
Zhang Deyang
https://www.telegraph.co.uk/news/worldnews/asia/
    china/12163417/Chinese-man-staged-his-own-funeral-
    just-to-see-how-many-people-would-turn-up.html
Vuk Peric
https://www.mentalfloss.com/article/91126/11-people-
    who-turned-alive-their-own-funeral

David Baerten
https://news.sky.com/story/tiktoker-fakes-his-own-
    death-to-find-out-who-cares-and-then-shows-up-at-
    the-funeral-12902143
Famous Legacies
https://community.thriveglobal.com/leaders-who-left-
    the-biggest-legacies/

Epilogue Story
https://www.creativeyouthideas.com/resources/teaching-
    illustrations/the-pear-tree-and-the-seasons-of-life/

Other References
John Naish writing in the *Daily Mail*, June 2023
Dr Dang Wei (JAA Heart Failure July 2023)
Hedva Hakin Technion-Israel Institute of Technology
Gerald Zamponi at the University of Calgary (2020)
Imperial College London (2020)
Carmine Pariante, Professor of Biological Psychiatry at
    King's College London
Society of Occupational Medicine (2023)
University College London *European Health Journal*
    (2023)
Finnish Institute for Health and Welfare (1987–2007)
Dr Cathy Stannard writing in the *Daily Mail*, June 2023
The Cochrane Research Body Australian Study (2015)
University Hospital North Study Norway (2023)
Arizona State University Study (2013)
Harvard University (1988)
University of London as part of UK Household
    Longitudinal survey (2011–2020)

Acknowledgements

- **John Winstanley** helped me shape the original content and focus of the book.
- **Peter Chester** kept me in his sights by offering insights into various aspects of the book's development.
- **Julie Cole** gladly read each part of the book as I was writing it and continues to support me.
- **Mike Potts** wrote the foreword and is someone who has championed my cause.
- **Richard Ellis**, my next-door neighbour, brought a business-style approach to the book and is probably the polar opposite to me which I think is a good thing when you're creating your tribe.
- **Rosie Lowe** saw something in me and my ramblings that she could harness with The Book Guild.

Words of Wisdom from the Contributors

- **Richard Bamford** – "Stress is a useless emotion, especially if you can't influence or change the cause."
- **Julie Cole** – "Don't have a set way of dealing with things. Judge each situation on its own merits and act accordingly."
- **Fred Eyre** – "Don't make any promises you can't keep."
- **Bryan Gray CBE** – "Two thoughts have guided me all my business and personal life: where there is no vision, the people perish and everyone has talents, but we may need help to reveal them."
- **Professor Barry Hymer** – "Hero-worship no one. Envy no one. Never underestimate anyone. Believe in the extraordinary potential of everyone."
- **Mark Lawrenson** – "Don't kiss your granny while she's shaving."
- **Dr Peter Lumsden** – "At the end of the day, we rarely feel we've achieved all we wanted to. But it's okay!"
- **Don Macpherson** – "Keep going, keep helping others: maybe you can't help everybody, but never forget to help yourself as this will help you help others, this is selfish, and it is a necessary quality."

- **Jenny Pelling** – "My favourite two are stay curious and never stop learning and in times of self-doubt, ask yourself, what would Beyoncé do?"
- **Tony Scholes** – "Never assume."
- **Derek Shaw** – "Every pound is a prisoner."
- **Mel Tottoh** – "Always believe in the positive power and potential of the human condition."
- **Steve Warner** – "As a dyslexic leader, don't criticise me for my wonderful imaginative spelling, but praise me for my big thinking."
- **Richard Askam** – "Time is precious. Give it freely. There's no greater gift."
- **Oshor Williams** – "Everyone has a story, and everyone has a value, so in this life strive to be a contributor not just a beneficiary."
- **Mark Beaumont** – "Be valued for who you are, not just what you do."

About the Author

After failing all his O-level exams in 1977, Ross left school and went through ten years of learning to prove to himself, and to others, that he was academically capable. For the following eight years, on his road to self-discovery, he was exploring his potential and searching for his place in the world. He had many jobs; bingo caller, road digger, nightshift worker in a beer production company, property developer, self-employed events manager and food outlet owner.

For the past thirty-five years though, Ross has diligently pursued his own focused professional development, credibility and acceptance. He has found and nurtured this expertise as a commercial manager in professional football; teacher, lecturer and international coach; corporate and educational trainer, MHFA trainer; lead consultant in education, health and well-being; online learning programme generator; keynote speaker; TV, radio guest and author.

In this time, he has developed potential and belief within children, young adults and senior established professionals. He has worked in several countries with individuals and teams of various ages, abilities, motivations and aspirations. He is now an established leader in mindset, mental health and performance. In his lifetime to date, through his keynote speaking, training and published writing, he has probably changed the lives of over a million people.

All of this is juxtaposed against adapting to physical, physiological, and emotional disability. It has made his life feel like a grind at times. *"You will always find me sitting down somewhere"* seems to be an appropriate subheading to his life and his disabilities have made him think and act differently.

Now in his sixties, the journey is still unfinished. His remaining two goals are to reach his own potential and to gently support others, and in so doing, provide a legacy in memory of his late parents who instilled a kindness and awareness of others' needs within him.

His authentic and experienced 'wisdoms' speak directly to people. He doesn't know all the answers, but it is this quest for reaching his own potential whilst helping others that drives Ross on.

"As my life has been more ordinary than extraordinary, the lessons I have learnt may be highly relatable to others. Experience teaches you that we are always growing, and wisdom from life is knowing how and when to apply this understanding."

Ross McWilliam
BA Hons, MSc Coaching, PGCE, CMI Level 7,
MHFA England
ross@rossmcwilliam.com

www.cuppajourney.com
www.mindsetpro.co.uk

Want More Sonoma Learning?